YEARNING
FOR
YESTERDAY

YEARNING
FOR
YESTERDAY

A SOCIOLOGY OF NOSTALGIA

Fred Davis

THE FREE PRESS
A Division of Macmillan Publishing Co., Inc.
NEW YORK

Collier Macmillan Publishers
LONDON

The Free Press
A Division of Macmillan Publishing Co., Inc.
866 Third Avenue, New York, N.Y. 10022

Collier Macmillan Canada, Ltd.

Library of Congress Catalog Card Number: 78-19838

Printed in the United States of America

printing number

1 2 3 4 5 6 7 8 9 10

Library of Congress Cataloging in Publication Data

Davis, Fred
   Yearning for yesterday.

      Includes index.
      1. Nostalgia. 2. Personality. 3. Arts--Psychologi-
cal aspects. 4. United States--Popular culture.
I. Title.
BF575.N6D38   1979   301.1   78-19838
ISBN 0-02-906950-5

TABLE OF CONTENTS

PREFACE

That someone other than a poet or psychologist should write of nostalgia may seem presumptous as well as surprising. Consider, however, that nostalgia, despite its private, sometimes intensely felt personal character, is a deeply social emotion as well. By this I mean that, like many other feelings and thoughts we experience, nostalgia derives from and has continuing implications for our lives as social actors. It leads us to search among remembrances of persons and places of our past in an effort to bestow meaning upon persons and places of our present (and to some degree our future). A *sociology* of nostalgia, therefore, is concerned with tracking down the sources of nostalgic experience in group life and determining what general relevance and meaning nostalgia has for our present life and, somewhat more abstractly, what consequences it has for society as a whole. This sociology is in some part what I try to accomplish in this book, although as you will perhaps too readily become aware, the omissions are staggering and some of the questions raised are more complex than the few simple ones for which I propose answers.

This is a book not about nostalg*ias*—specific fashions, crazes, and fads that seem endlessly to crop up—but about a

general phenomenon. I think it important to state this because in gathering materials for this study I would almost
invariably be asked to give reasons for the resurgence of
interest in the romantic comedy movies of the thirties; the
rediscovered attachment to swing bands and ocean cruises,
which obviously harks back to the period immediately before
the Second World War; the revival of literary interest in F.
Scott Fitzgerald (and the loss of interest in his rival, Ernest
Hemingway); the nostalgic Beatlemania of the late seventies,
barely half a decade after the foursome dominated the
world's popular music scene; and so forth. The way these
requests usually were framed seemed to imply that something
inherent in those phenomona made them candidates for a
nostalgic revival *at this particular time* ("The M.G.M. thirties'
comedies were so witty and charming, whereas nowadays
there's so little wit and charm in what we see on TV or at
the movies"). This viewpoint is fundamentally a faulty formulation of nostalgia's causal chain. It is incorrect to suppose
that qualities associated with some slice of the past "cause"
the nostalgia we feel today.

Even were the implicit formulation not in error—although
the nature of the error itself is revealing of some facets of
nostalgia—it still would be virtually impossible to give *specific*
reasons for specific nostalgias other than that "it" (in the
vernacular) "caught on" whereas some other "it" from the
past, which might equally have served as a fit object for
nostalgia, may not even have surfaced—possibly because
those with an interest in promoting nostalgic revivals never
got around to thinking of the other "it." As with so many
phenomena in the realm of popular taste, the vagaries of nostalgic success, survival, and revival are of awesome dimension.

Almost anything from our past can emerge as an object of
nostalgia, provided that we can somehow view it in a pleasant
light. (This effectively eliminates from nostalgia's universe
such grotesque possibilities as a "nostalgia" for the ovens at
Auschwitz or for the bomb at Hiroshima.) What is important

for us therefore, and what this book aims to develop, is an understanding of the *general* conditions and circumstances that evoke nostalgic feeling, not the largely adventitious occurrences associated with the success of one or another specific nostalgic manifestation. (The latter interest falls more properly in the domain of study dealing with promotion, publicity, and propaganda in modern society: mass-communications analysis. As such, it is in its essential features hardly distinguishable from any reasoned inquiry seeking, for example, to account for the market success of a popular song, a household product, or a political candidate.)

In the course of gathering material for this study I interviewed, with the help of an open-ended interview guide of my own design, some twelve persons in the hope of learning from them what their nostalgic experiences were like and what, in general, nostalgia meant to them. For essentially similar purposes I also administered a brief, much more topically circumscribed questionnaire, also of my own design, to students in several of my university classes. Hence, here and there in the book I speak of "the respondent," of "my informants," or of "those I interviewed." Lest false inferences be drawn from the use of these terms, let me state that I in no way wish anyone to presume that what follows is an empirical study in the conventional social-survey (or, for that matter, ethnographic) sense. My resort to a small number of almost casually selected interviewees and questionnaire respondents was designed solely to jog my thoughts and fuel my ruminations on the topic of nostalgia and, in one or two instances, to establish or negate some rather unrefined proposition—for example, does *everyone* associate nostalgia with homesickness? Is the experience of nostalgia *ever* so painful that persons seek actively to avoid it? But none of what I learned from these survey-like forays into the area can be taken as establishing representativeness in even a remote sense of that word. I clearly intend this book to be an essayistic inquiry into the subject of nostalgia rather than a report of empirical findings pertaining to it.

Nostalgia is much in vogue these days, so much so that hundreds of curio shops bear its name and many a person has begun to move beyond simply indulging it to musing openly on what the vogue is about. Befitting its prominence as a kind of disposition of contemporary collective life, the French actress Simone Signoret has even chosen to name her book of reminiscences after the (probably anonymous) wry vintage observation that nostalgia is no longer what it used to be.[1] Whether it is or isn't, and what accounts for ours being so nostalgic an era are central concerns of this book. Without giving all of the plot away this soon in the story, as it were, suffice it say that the current nostalgia boom must be understood in terms of its close relationship to the era of social upheaval that preceded it. It, too, then can be expected to pass, although before it expires in history I would hope that studies such as this might help us to understand nostalgia for the quintessentially human thing it is and to neither revile it, as do many on the left, nor succumb abjectly to it, as do many on the right.

---

[1] Simone Signoret, *Nostalgia Isn't What It Used to Be* (New York: Harper & Row, 1978).

ACKNOWLEDGMENTS

I welcome the opportunity given me to acknowledge the many (for the most part unreciprocated) debts which the pursuit and consummation of such a work entail. Among those who were good enough to offer me their thoughts and insights on the topic, including those who commented on earlier chapter drafts, I wish especially to thank my wife, Marcella; Murray Davis; Joseph Gusfield; Chandra Mukerji; Virginia Olesen; and Anselm Strauss. I owe a special debt to Gladys Topkis of The Free Press for her consistently sage and exquisitely informed editorial advice. Most of all there are two persons, unknown to each other, who bear so special a relationship to what follows that I trust they will think well enough of it to associate themselves with it as much as I would like them to. One is my old and very dear friend from graduate student days at the University of Chicago, Gerald Handel. Through the force of his sociological intelligence and insight, not only did he encourage me to persevere when my enthusiasms (and ideas) flagged, but from across a continent he supplied me with a constant stream of nostalgia-rich clippings from that newspaper not quite like any other, the *New York Times*. The other is my friend and former secretary, Vicki Peguillan, who through her sheer enthusiasm for the topic and her extraordinary ability to articulate and reflect upon her own nostalgic experiences made it, in some broader human sense, all seem very worthwhile.

YEARNING
FOR
YESTERDAY

In Penny Lane the barber shaves another customer,
We see the banker sitting waiting for a trim,
And then the fireman rushes in
From the pouring rain,
Very strange.

Penny Lane is in my ears and in my eyes,
There beneath the blue suburban skies
I sit. And meanwhile back . . . .

The Beatles, "Penny Lane,"
from the Album Magical
Mystery Tour, *Capitol*
EMI *Records #2835*

THE NOSTALGIC EXPERIENCE:
WORDS AND MEANINGS

WE WISH FIRST TO CONSIDER the experience, its shapes and attitudes. But because it is a named thing, and because with such things the name itself is so much a part of the experience, we must begin with the word.

Nostalgia is from the Greek *nostos,* to return home, and *algia,* a painful condition—thus, a painful yearning to return home. Coined by the Swiss physician Johannes Hofer[1] in the late seventeenth century, the term was meant to designate a familiar, if not especially frequent, condition of extreme homesickness among Swiss mercenaries fighting far from their native land in the legions of one or another European despot. The "symptoms" of those so afflicted were said by Hofer and other learned physicians of the time to be despondency, melancholia, lability of emotion, including

---

[1] Johannes Hofer, "Medical Dissertation on Nostalgia," first published in 1688 in Latin and translated into English by Carolyn K. Anspach, *Bulletin of the History of Medicine* 2 (1934): 376–391.

profound bouts of weeping, anorexia, a generalized "wasting away," and, not infrequently, attempts at suicide. It is of interest to note in passing that to the medical mind of the early Enlightment such humble, straightforward terms as the German *heimweh,* the English *homesickness* and the French *maladie du pays* were somehow found wanting; a *disease* had to be invented to replace what up until that time had, we can assume, been regarded as an unfortunate though familiar vicissitude of life. And no sooner did the condition receive benefit of a diagnostic category than numerous physicians, particularly ones with military affiliations, undertook the search to discover the nature and site of the organic lesion associated with the disease, as either cause or effect thereof, and in numerous eighteenth- and nineteenth-century medical tracts on the subject somewhat indistinguishably as both.[2]

Hofer himself, for example, speculated that a principal cause of the disease was "the quite continuous vibration of animal spirits through those fibers of the middle brain in which impressed traces of ideas of the Fatherland still cling."[3]

Some years later, in 1731, another German-Swiss physician, J. J. Scheuchzer, suggested the disease—that it was a "disease" seemed no longer open to question—was due to the sufferer's having experienced a sharp differential in atmospheric pressure causing excessive body pressurization, which in turn drove blood from the heart to the brain, thereby producing the observed affliction of sentiment.[4] How else to

[2] For an excellent and very comprehensive summary of learned thought and writing on the topic of nostalgia from Hofer to the mid-twentieth century, see Charles A. A. Zwingmann "'Heimweh' or 'Nostalgic Reaction': A Conceptual Analysis and Interpretation of a Medico-Psychological Phenomenon," unpublished Ph.D. dissertation, School of Education, Stanford University, 1959.

[3] Hofer, "Medical Dissertation on Nostalgia," p. 384.

[4] Zwingmann, "'Heimweh' or 'Nostalgic Reaction'," pp. 20–21, It is fascinating to observe how, despite the almost charming implausibility of Scheuchzer's theory, nearly all theories of nostalgia, from the most mechanistic and physiological to the most existential and psychological, draw on some notion of sudden alteration, sharp transition, or marked discontinuity in life experience to explain the

account for the fact that the disease seemed to be so peculiarly an affliction of *Swiss* soldiers? Were they not alone
among European soldiers in experiencing the precipitous
descent from high Alpine climes to the plains of France,
Saxony, Prussia, and the Low Countries? Of course, with the
development of mass armies and the introduction of universal
conscription by European states in the late eighteenth and
nineteenth centuries it was soon "discovered" that soldiers
of other countries on military duty far from home were
equally subject to the disease. But up to the time roughly of
the Napoleonic wars the view persisted that the Swiss alone
were *specially* vulnerable to the disease. Some military
physicians even went so far as to suggest that it might be
induced by neurological damage to eardrum and brain cell
caused by exposure to the incessant clanging of cowbells in
the rarefied Alpine atmosphere.[5]

Despite the diverse, often bizarre scientistic pretensions of
the many military physicians who interested themselves in
the subject,[6] it appears that well into the modern era the

---

phenomenon. Without further distracting the reader with such
matters here, they are nonetheless forewarned that in this book I,
too, intend with some modifications to work this vein, albeit from a
sociological angle.

[5] *Ibid.*, pp. 19–20.

[6] Indeed, according to the evidence provided by Zwingmann, *ibid.*,
pp. 1–179, during the eighteenth and nineteenth centuries the
medical interest in the "disease" nostalgia was confined almost
exclusively to doctors in the military or those closely associated
with it. As a sort of footnote to both the sociology of knowledge
and the sociology of medicine, it is perhaps not amiss to speculate
that the "disease" was discovered (more like invented) at the time it
was because of the problematic and costly *social* character of the
condition to which it referred. After all, *nostalgia* in the context of
military service can mean lowered troop morale, malingering,
desertion, defeat in battle, and, ultimately, loss of national wealth
and prestige. In civilian life it is perceived as affecting individuals
alone, who, unlike soldiers or sailors, are rarely so situated as to be
highly "contagious" to others. In any event, even if it could be
shown that the social costs of *homesickness* in civil society were
ultimately as great as those of nostalgia in the armed forces, the
negative consequences of the latter are clearly more vivid, im-

3

strong semantic bond between the disease category nostalgia and some commonsensical notion of homesickness remained largely intact. It was only with the word's unmooring from its pathological base, with its demilitarization and demedicalization, as it were, that it began to acquire many of the connotations it has today. Judging from Zwingmann's careful review and from the entries in the Oxford English Dictionary, this could not have happened much before the turn of the present century, for it is only then, and most notably in America, that one begins to find scholarly reports of a medical or psychological sort that neither treat the condition as a "disease" in the conventional medical sense nor limit its incidence to persons in the military. But once introduced into popular parlance, the process of semantic drift has proved so pronounced that nowadays only a minority of speakers, as Zwingmann's and my own informal surveys of college students attest, are likely to associate nostalgia with homesickness *per se*[7], while almost no one thinks of it as a "disease." On the contrary, most students are amused when told it was once regarded as such.

Not only does the word *nostalgia* appear to have been fully "demilitarized" and "demedicalized" by now but, with its rapid assimilation into American popular speech since roughly the nineteen-fifties,[8] it appears to be undergoing a

mediate, and possibly even more calculable in gross terms of retreat and defeat. Hence, the military's need to construct a disease category which in accord with the Enlightenment philosophy of the time would simultaneously remove the condition from the application of ineffective punitive sanctions while ostensibly rendering it amenable to scientific diagnosis, treatment, and cure. Cf. Thomas S. Szasz, *The Myth of Mental Illness* (New York: Harper, 1961), Part I, and Eliot Freidson, *Profession of Medicine* (New York: Dodd, Mead, 1970), Part I.

[7] The several dozen students I surveyed associated such words as *warm, old times, childhood,* and *yearning* with the term "nostalgia" much more frequently than they did *homesickness,* the latter being selected by only about half of them from a long checklist of possible associations.

[8] My sense is that until well into the nineteen-fifties *nostalgia* was regarded as a "fancy word." Easy and unself-conscious use of it was

process of "depsychologization" as well. By this I mean that whatever residual connotations of aberrance or mental malfunction—even of a minor or transitory character—may have clung to the word following its habitation of two centuries in the realm of psychiatry, these too are rapidly being dissipated through positively tinged popular and commercial usage. So easily and "naturally" does the word come to our tongues nowadays that it is much more likely to be classed with such familiar emotions as love, jealousy, and fear than with such "conditions" as melancholia, obsessive compulsion, or claustrophobia.

Thus, in seeking to understand the nature of the experience from an examination of the etymology of the word, we are confronted with a compound sociolinguistic paradox, to wit: (1) the drift of the word's contemporary connotations from the pathological and occupationally specialized meanings with which it was originally invested and (2) the gradual semantic deterioration of its core referent of *homesickness*. It is almost as if, once lifted from its original context, the word sought of its own accord that murky and inchoate amalgam of sentiments to which so homely a word as homesickness could no longer render symbolic justice.

But, before exploring the new realm of meaning, we may ask how it came to pass that the demedicalized word in the course of the twentieth century acquired such astonishing evocativeness and prominence while gradually shedding that core referent—homesickness—which once distinguished it? Short of the difficult, extensive, and tedious historical survey of the word's usages that would be necessary to answer the question fully, one can only speculate on some of the influences at play. In some small part, perhaps, the sheer phonetic symbolism of the word, its easy association with such like-sounding words as nocturnal and nosegay along with the "-algia" suggestion of malaise and mild affliction,

---

confined mainly to psychiatrists, academic psychologists, and relatively few cultivated lay speakers.

may have helped cloak it in allusive romantic imagery that had been lacking as long as the word was confined to a medical context. More important, probably, is the diminished existential salience of "home" in its concrete locational sense, and hence of "*home*sickness" *per se* in the modern world. As with so many other dimensions of what Karl Polanyi has termed "The Great Transformation,"[9] the passing of "home" in the old sense arises from the tremendous mobility of persons in their occupations, residences, localities, and even countries of birth that is characteristic of the industrial order of modern Western society. Increasingly, and at an almost frenetic pace by the mid-twentieth century, this constant movement in sociogeographic space has begun to dislodge man's deep psychological attachment to a specific house, in a specific locality, in a specific region, which over the centuries had been fostered by the more settled and protracted arrangements of a primarily agricultural and small-town society.

In short, *home* is no longer where the hearth is. This, of course, is not to say that for moderns the body of sentiments and images the term conveys no longer exists or is incapable of being experienced. Rather, it points simply to the marked severance of "home-type" sentiments from home *per se,* even if the four-letter word itself has retained many of its geographically specific connotations of place. (Home is always some *place*, be it ever so humble or grand, fixed or even movable, as in the case of modern trailers and mobile homes.) Because, then, home as such can for so many no longer evoke the "remembrance of things past" it once did, it has fallen to other words, "nostalgia" among them, to comprehend the sometimes pedestrian, sometimes disjunctive, and sometimes eerie sense we carry of our own past and of its meaning for present and future.

---

[9] Karl Polanyi, *The Great Transformation* (New York: Farrar & Rinehart, 1944).

If then it is no longer *home*sickness *per se* that is centrally or, for many, even peripherally summoned to mind when the word "nostalgia" is used in everyday speech, to what experience does the word point? How is it that I can speak the word and my listener will apparently understand what I mean, if only more or less or just sufficiently for the purpose of making conversation? At the very least my listener would, for example, sense that it signifies something more than mere memory of the past and something less than the "diseased state of mind" it once referred to. And, why is it, for example, that when someone tells me of a friend who is "feeling nostalgic" I know generally that the friend is neither elated nor in bleak despair, that his mood is more contemplative than active, that the echoes, if not always the actuality, of tears and laughter alternate more vividly in him at such a time than they do at other times? Obviously, and without foolishly claiming any precise, intrinsic, or immutable meaning for the word, there is *some* common experiential base to which the word points and which it *qua* word evokes. And this can be said despite the incorporeality of nostalgia's referent or the fact that, as words go, it is in the Jamesian sense a heavily fringed word and therefore susceptible to semantic vagueness, drift, and ambiguity.[10]

These difficulties and qualifications notwithstanding, we must now return to our abandoned beginning; we must move from the word to "the thing"—which is to say the contents, contours, and contexts of that contemporary *experience* (it was something different in the past and will probably be different again in the future)—which the word, however variably and gropingly, refers to. In short, we must now probe that special experience which, intensely private and subjective as it may be, leads "most of us most of the time" to employ the word "nostalgia" rather than some other word or no word at all.

[10] William James, *Psychology: The Briefer Course* (New York: Harper torchbooks, 1961), pp. 30–42.

YEARNING FOR YESTERDAY
Nostalgia and the Past

Banal though the statement may appear, it still needs saying: if there is one thing upon which all agree—from those who have only momentarily reflected on the phenomenon to those who have devoted much time to its study—it is that the material of nostalgic experience is the past. Moreover, the weight of testimony seems to suggest (we shall have more to say on this later) that the past which is the object of nostalgia must in some fashion be a personally experienced past rather than one drawn solely, for example, from chronicles, almanacs, history books, memorial tablets, or, for that matter, legend. (Can I be nostalgic for the Ganges, a place I have never seen, or you for the Crusades, a time when you have never lived?)

At the outset, therefore, it would seem important to distinguish nostalgic from antiquarian feeling, a condition with which it is sometimes confused. One may, for example, feel a powerful identification with the American Revolution, be extremely knowledgeable regarding it, and even entertain a strong wish to have lived then rather than now. But can one feel *nostalgia* for it? Of course, there are those who insist that this is precisely what they feel, going so far as to claim that their yearning for the period of Washington and Jefferson is every bit as vivid and intimate as another's is for the songs and friends of his youth. Who are we to dispute the claim, especially since in matters of feeling words to a considerable extent can be made to mean whatever one wants them to mean? Indeed, in light of the word's great vogue in recent years, it is conceivable that "nostalgia" *qua* word will in time acquire connotations that extend its meaning to *any* sort of positive feeling toward *anything* past, no matter how remote or historical. For now, however, I believe it is still the case that most speakers would assign a story-derived enchantment with Revolutionary America to a different category of experience from the one they reserve for fondly remembered material from their own lives. Paradoxically, this is perhaps because the active antiquarian mood grants greater existential license to the imagination and permits more pure self-fantasy than does the memory of events and places from our own lives. However profligate our reconstructions of the latter may be, in the end the memory of them is constrained by, at minimum, some nagging unspoken sense of the way things "*actually* were then." This, too, may help account for the note of wistfulness in nostalgia's attitude, which antiquarian feeling does not encompass.

Still other ambiguities and possible confusions surround the apparently simple assertion that the material of nostalgic experience is the past. Additional clarifications and qualifications are in order.

First, it should be made clear that to claim that nostalgic material derives from a personally experienced past is not to claim that the past "causes" or even "explains" current nostalgia or, more precisely, that it is the motivational source or triggering circumstance for a nostalgic experience as such. On the contrary, since our awareness of the past, our summoning of it, our very knowledge that it *is* past, can be nothing other than present experience, what occasions us to feel nostalgia must also reside in the present, regardless of how much the ensuing nostalgic experience may draw its sustenance from our memory of the past. Inasmuch as any serious student of the phenomenon is bound to stumble quickly upon this recognition, it is not surprising to find researchers like Nawas and Platt, for example, proposing (though not altogether persuasively, I believe) a "future-oriented theory of nostalgia," in which they maintain that the condition represents a mild, neurotically displaced "concern over, or denial of, the future. . .rather than a 'homing instinct' or a reaction to unsuccessful adaptation to one's present surroundings."[11] Similarly, Zwingmann con-

[11] M. Mike Nawas and Jerome J. Platt, "A Future Oriented Theory of Nostalgia," *Journal of Individual Psychology* 21 (May 1965): 55.

ceives of the nostalgic experience as essentially a normal psychological reaction triggered by fear of actual or impending change.[12] But whether nostalgia be healthy or neurotic, present- or future-oriented, these authors are clearly correct in temporally differentiating the motivational springs of nostalgia from its ideational and imagistic contents.

I dwell on this matter because it is very common for commentators to "explain" a current wave of nostalgia for, to cite some recent examples, "the fifties," "the pre-TV Hollywood musical," "the radio serials of the thirties," "the clothing fashions of the First World War," and so forth, by appealing to certain putative attributes of the period or style in question and showing how it was allegedly superior, more fulfilling, or more fathomable than what exists today. (Such "explanations" do not explain at all; in effect they do little more than extend and intellectually elaborate the essence of the nostalgic expression itself.) Thus, even so knowledgeable an observer of contemporary culture as Robert Nisbet, despite a fleeting insight to the effect that nostalgia tells us more about present moods than about past realities, explains the current wave of nostalgia for the thirties by what he sees as the more positive moral and civic tone obtaining then, e.g., the humor in the midst of economic adversity, the deep belief in the eventual efficacy of social reform, the sense of participation in contrast to the present mood of alienation.[13] Whether such collective virtues were present during the thirties in the degree claimed is, at best, debatable—others still see the period as one of unmitigated chaos and disillusionment—but to regard them as the *reason* for our nostalgic evocation of that era is surely to confuse consequence with cause. Whatever in our present situation evokes it, nostalgia *uses the past*—falsely, accurately, or, as I shall later

---

[12] Zwingmann, "'Heimweh' or 'Nostalgic Reaction'," p. 204.

[13] Robert Nisbet, "The 1930's: America's Major Nostalgia," *The Key Reporter* 38, no. 1 (Autumn 1972): 2-4.

maintain, in specially reconstructed ways—but it is not the product thereof.[14]

A second concern stemming from the claim, perhaps no longer so obvious, that the material of nostalgia is the past comes down essentially to the heraclitean paradox: how far past must past be before it is experienced as past? Recently a friend remarked of another friend, much to the amusement of those present, "She's so nostalgic, she's nostalgic for yesterday." The humor in the observation suggests, of course, that there is—or somehow should be—some necessary passage of time before the events of our lives come to serve as objects of nostalgia. But if one day is too soon and if, as I implied earlier, that which extends beyond the span of one's own lifetime is too removed, where do we draw the line—a month, a year, a decade, a generation? Without becoming mired in metaphysical musings on the enigmatic topic of time, it is perhaps worth suggesting for now that more is involved than the mere passage of clock-time. Lived-time (or *durée* in the Bergsonian sense) is more important for an understanding of nostalgia,[15] and, as I shall develop further in the chapter on "Nostalgia and the Life Cycle," it is the subjective contrast of succeeding "identity gestalts" that facilitates the resort to nostalgic activity. Put differently, the ability to feel nos-

---

[14] Paralleling Bartlett's now classic critique of theories that conceive of memory as an accretion of fixed and inert thought traces inscribed on the brain by prior experience, I, too, would question approaches that view nostalgia as more a by-product of the past than an emergent from the present. Barlett's processual view of memory as an "effort after meaning" more closely appoximates my own view of nostalgia, albeit with the recognition that nostalgic experience constitutes a special kind of memory or "effort after meaning," one with its own distinctive cognitive-emotional structure. See F. C. Bartlett, *Remembering* (Cambridge, England: Cambridge University Press, 1932).

[15] For an excellent discussion of the difference between clock-time and *durée*, see Alfred Schutz, "On Multiple Realities," in *Collected Papers, Volume I: The Problem of Social Reality* (The Hague: Martin Nijhoff, 1962), pp. 207-259.

talgia for events in our past has less (although clearly something) to do with how recent or distant these events are than with the way they contrast—or, more accurately, the way we *make* them contrast—with the events, moods, and dispositions of our present circumstances.[16] (Again, though, the reader must be cautioned that it is not contrast *per se* but rather *certain kinds* of subjective contrasts that engender the stuff of nostalgia.)

Finally, to round out this discussion of nostalgia's relation to the past, some consideration should be given to the logical, if intuitively incongruous, question of whether it is possible to feel nostalgia for the future. (The late Mayor Richard E. Daley once assured Chicagoans in an often-quoted remark: "I am looking to the future with nostalgia.") Oddly enough, several people I interviewed said it was possible. On closer questioning, however, it turned out they meant that they could, and sometimes did, envision themselves at a relatively distant point in the future looking back nostalgically on events that were imminent or whose occurrence could be anticipated "in the normal course" of the life career. Thus a young woman, for example, said she imagined herself a grandmother looking back nostalgically on the infancy of her daughters-to-be. Significantly, the distinguishing "looking back" feature of nostalgia is retained in this forward projection of an as yet unrealized state. Moreover, the state itself—and herein nostalgia acquires considerable sociological significance—is often of a highly conventional cast, e.g., marriage, children, job success, a home of one's own.[17] These

---

[16] An early, though poorly developed prototype of this formulation was suggested by Beardsley Ruml, an important business figure of the thirties and forties who, besides serving as head of Macy's, came to be known primarily as the father of the distinctly "non-nostalgic" federal withholding tax. See his sensitive and broadly conceived piece, "Some Notes on Nostalgia" *Saturday Review of Literature*, June 22, 1946, pp. 7-9.

[17] See the brilliant analysis of this topic in the classic essay "Memory and Childhood Amnesia" (1947) in Ernest G. Schactel, *Metamorphosis* (New York: Basic Books, 1959).

are the institutional staples which we are socialized to contemplate from an early age and which, indeed, we are required to anticipate if there is to be cultural continuity between generations. To suggest, however, that such "future imaginings of conventionalized pasts" attest to some hidden facility of nostalgia to "feel forward" in time in much the same fashion as it "feels backward" would be to falsify a key attribute of the experience.

The "Special" Past of Nostalgia

But if nostalgia, as it is experienced in today's world by users of the word, locates its objects and events in the past, how does it differ from a variety of other subjective states that are equally, and perhaps even more strongly oriented to the past? History, rememberance, recollection, reminiscence, revivification, and recall are but a few of the words in our language that somehow denote the mental state of a sentient being looking back in time. And yet we sense that, however they may differ among themselves (and of course they do), none conveys quite the same feeling tone as does "nostalgia," the difference being more substantial than the formal hairsplitting of those semanticists who claim that no two words are alike and there is no such thing as a true synonym. Thus, for example, merely to remember the places of our youth is not the same as to feel nostalgic over them; nor does even active reminiscence—however happy, benign, or tortured its content—necessarily capture the subjective state we associate with nostalgic feeling.

Clearly, more than "mere past" is involved. It is a past imbued with special qualities, which, moreover, acquires its significance from the particular way we juxtapose it to certain features of our present lives. Two points need to be made in this connection, even though, as we shall see later in this chapter in our discussion of "The Ascending Orders

13

of Nostalgia," both are subject to numerous complications, which I shall disregard here. The first is that no matter how one later comes to reevaluate that piece of past which is the object of his notalgia—or, for that matter, irrespective of how he may later choose to interpret the meaning of the nostalgic experience itself—the nostalgic feeling is infused with imputations of past beauty, pleasure, joy, satisfaction, goodness, happiness, love, and the like, in sum, any or several of the *positive* affects of being. Nostalgic feeling is almost never infused with those sentiments we commonly think of as negative—for example, unhappiness, frustration, despair, hate, shame, abuse. To paraphrase several of those I interviewed:

> I mostly get nostalgic over the nice, pleasant and fun things in my past. The unpleasant things I've either forgotten, or when something reminds me of them I drive them out of mind. But I never feel nostalgic about them.

Some will, to be sure, allow that their nostalgia is tinged frequently with a certain sadness or even melancholy but are then inclined to describe it as "a nice sort of sadness"—"bittersweet" is an apt word occasionally used. The implication is that the component of sadness serves only to heighten the quality of recaptured joy or contentment. (Note how far all this is from the word's original sense of "aggravated homesickness.") Indeed, the nostaltic mood is one whose active tendency is to envelop all that may have been painful or unattractive about the past in a kind of fuzzy, redeemingly benign aura. The hurts, the annoyances, disappointments, and irritations, if they are permitted to intrude at all, are filtered forgivingly through an "it-was-all-for-the-best" attitude or, at the very least, are patronized under some "great human comedy" metaphor.

The special place accorded the "beauteous" past of nostalgia in feeling and action is further attested to by the fact that, in English at least, there exists no antonym for it, no word to describe feelings of rejection or revulsion toward one's past or some segment thereof. It would, of course, be easy enough to coin such a term much as Hofer did "nostalgia" some three centuries ago: *nostophobia,* an abnormal fear or dislike of home, immediately suggests itself as an exact opposite. Yet no such word has come into use despite the fact that millions upon millions would freely confess feelings of unrelieved sadness, regret, and disillusionment toward events, persons, and places from the past, with some even extending the claim to "everything that happened to me up until I left home." There are others who take a certain pride in proclaiming, almost as a sign of mental health or moral superiority, that the past holds no interest for them whatsoever; their only concern is with the present and future. In any event, negative affect toward the lived past, be it of either the episodic or chronic variety, seems not to crystallize itself subjectively *qua* emotion in quite the same distinctive or recognizable way as does its opposite, nostalgia. It is hard to know to what to attribute this asymmetry, but it does suggest that *nostalgia,* unlike its imaginary opposite *nostophobia,* may feed in part at least on vestigial ethological traces in man of what has sometimes been termed "the homing instinct." Perhaps because of this it acquires a distinctive emotional "tone," the equivalent of which is absent from whatever complex of affects "nostophobia" could be imagined to comprise.

The second point bearing on nostalgia's special relationship to the past has to do with the relatively sharp contrast that the experience casts on present circumstances and conditions, which, compared to the past, are invariably felt to be, and often *reasoned* to be as well, more bleak, grim, wretched, ugly, deprivational, unfulfilling, frightening, and so forth.[18] Or, should these adjectives strike one as possibly too accented a description of the dark side of nostalgic experience, then cold, gray, unpromising, unengaging, and uninspiring. Either way—and no matter how the "good past/bad present" contrast may later come to be discounted, discarded, or

[18] Cf. Ruml, "Some Notes on Nostalgia."

transmuted—evidently it is requisite for this inner dialogue to have been struck before it can be said that a nostalgic experience has occurred. Indeed, so characteristic is this of nostalgic experience that it can perhaps be regarded as its distinctive rhetorical signature. Of course, none of this implies anything—and I shall have much more to say on this later—about the actuality of a beautiful past and a grim present. We are here wholly concerned with the *subjective,* cognitive-emotional set of nostalgia and seek to understand it in its own right without getting embroiled in tedious discussions of whether what nostalgia claims for past and present is "really the case."

To conceive of nostalgic experience as encompassing some necessary inner dialogue between past *and* present is not to suggest that the two sides in the dialogue are of equal strength, independence, or resonance or that there is even any serious doubt over which way the conversation is destined to go. While both speakers must be present and engaged, as it were, for nostalgia's mise-en-scène to fall into place, in the ensuing dialogue it is *always* the adoration of the past that triumphs over lamentations for the present. Indeed, this is the whole point of the dialogue; for to permit present woes to douse the warm glow from the past is to succumb to melancholy or, worse yet, depression. And, while it may be true that the nostalgic dialogue nearly always entails some risk of this sort to the self, there can be no question that points at issue are intended to arrive at the foregone conclusion of the superiority of times and things past.

The Ascending Orders of Nostalgia

As with most things human, nostalgia soon comes to be complicated and confounded by a variety of cognitive and emotional qualifiers. This is so because man is a reflexive being; whatever set of conditions may have occasioned his nostalgic (or, for that matter, any other) reaction, he does not merely "react" and leave it at that. From time to time, at least, he is wont to question the reaction, examine it more closely, interpret it, and, perhaps, even consciously seek to manipulate its occurrence or outcome. In so doing he of course alters the quality of the "simple" experience, imparting to it new features, perspectives, and tensions. Thus, to feel nostalgia for something in one's past is not the *same* experience as to contemplate the nostalgia one feels for that something. Nor is either the *same* as, for example, some later questioning of the necessity to contemplate the experience at all rather than, let us say, indulge it to the full.

Of course the mind soon boggles under the burden of successive reflexivities of this kind. Moreover, there probably is some tendency for the more recessed frames, since they are farther removed from our primary experience, to harbor fragments of feelings and images that from individual to individual are quite ephemeral, highly privatized, and idiosyncratic—so much so that generalizations regarding their source or function are extremely difficult to make. Yet there appear to be at least two or three successive orders of nostalgic reaction that are sufficiently common in everyday experience to warrant an attempt to differentiate them. By "order of nostalgic reaction" I mean something other than the purely logical possibilities inherent in some such scheme as: I feel nostalgia; I reflect upon the nostalgia I feel; I reflect upon the reflection of the nostalgia I feel, etc. Rather, I shall point to three successive orders of cognition and emotion, the patternings of which derive not from the mere mechanical extension of ordinal possibilities but from the musings attendant on the course of life experience. I shall call these *First Order* or *Simple Nostalgia, Second Order* or *Reflexive Nostalgia,* and *Third Order* or *Interpreted Nostalgia.*

First Order or *Simple Nostalgia*: In line with the definition of nostalgia I have developed thus far, namely a positively toned evocation of a lived past in the context of some negative feeling toward present or impending circumstance, "Simple Nostalgia" is that subjective state which harbors the largely unexamined belief that THINGS WERE BETTER (MORE BEAUTIFUL) (HEALTHIER) (HAPPIER) (MORE CIVILIZED) (MORE EXCITING) *THEN* THAN *NOW*. In short, it is a more or less unabashed assertion of "The Beautiful Past and the Unattractive Present," notwithstanding the frequent tendency with such assertions to concede almost ritualistically (as if to impart an air of objectivity to their utterance) that people then, too, had problems and experienced hardships, usually followed by an inner feeling or spoken phrase beginning, "But despite this . . ." Some characteristic examples of Simple Nostalgia chosen at random from a variety of sources follow. From an interview with a young woman:

> When I think of the time my grandma was a girl I think of riding big-wheeled bicycles, wearing a long dress with a buckle in the back. I think of it as a romantic time. Then cars weren't around so much, but transportation was pretty good. You could get places. They had ocean liners. So you weren't really stuck in the same place like you were a hundred years ago. You could still move around, but you didn't have these huge urbanized areas like you have now with no open space and with people living atop each other.

From the observations of a psychiatrist appearing in Studs Terkel's book on the American memory of the Depression:

> Thirty, forty years ago people felt burdened by an excess of conscience. An excess of guilt and wrongdoing. In those days, regardless of impoverishment, there was more constraint on behavior. I cannot imagine looting thirty-five years ago. Despite want, the patterns of authority prevailed. Today, those standards have exploded. Looting and rioting have become sanctioned behavior in many communities. . . . [Then] the way of life was an established one. It did not explode in chaotic fashion. Despite deprivations, there was predictablity. You could make long-term plans. If you were willing to work your ass off you could look forward to reward ten years hence. Even during the Depression, there was more con-

tinuity in the way of life. Today there's no such conviction. People can't predict five years hence.[19]

From an article on life among the Beatniks in San Francisco's North Beach in the late nineteen-fifties:

I believe there was more communicating per square block in North Beach during the late fifties than there was in any other comparable place in America. More than anything else, language filled the streets. It floated down them in a bable and exploded in coffee shops and poetry readings, at private parties and public ones, like the great parties they used to throw at the Art Institute. And it even seeped out of the area to infect other parts of the city. San Francisco was ablaze and North Beach was the center of the bonfire.[20]

From a *New York Times* report on the dripless ice cream controversy—the speaker is president of an ice cream company that has thus far resisted the trend toward the dripless product:

"Ice cream is part of the new feeling of nostalgia, I think," Mr. Gaudrault said. "It reminds us of an old-fashioned period that we associate with wholesomeness and happy kids.

"Nobody ever got into trouble eating ice cream," he said, ignoring for the moment the plight of the nation's weight-watchers.[21]

From Herb Caen, the columnist for the *San Francisco Chronicle,* whose journalistic stock-in-trade is the sometimes tough guy–lachrymose, the sometimes ironic, and the sometimes almost mordant nostalgia for the city's past in light of the present era's "high-rise ugliness." Below he gives full vent to the Simple Nostalgic mode:

The last time San Francisco came roaring to life save for V-J Day (more mad than gay), was in the period immediately preceding the

---

[19] Studs Terkel, *Hard Times* (New York: Avon Books, 1970), p. 129.
[20] Jerry Kamstra, "Of Beats and Boo and North Beach in the Fifties," *Pacific Sun,* January 10–16, 1974, p. 21.
[21] Ernest Holsendolph, "I Scream, You Scream . . . Nostalgia Reinforced by No-Drip Ice Cream," Sunday *New York Times,* August 26, 1973, "News of the Week in Review" section, p. 12.

19

opening of the 1939 Exposition on Treasure Island. Men sprouted beards, women wore crinolines and bonnets, Polk St. became Polk Gulch and if you wandered into the area without at least a moustache, you were put into streetcorner cages, tried and fined. It was all done in high, festive spirit, and I doubt that the innocence (that is, the absence of violence) could ever be repeated. Although the thought went unspoken, that celebration marked the end of San Francisco's second childhood. War was on the horizon, and for many of the thousands who roamed the streets and ferried to Treasure Island, it was the last party as the end of an era. Something precious and tantalizingly idefinable disappeared forever, gone with the stately ferry boats, the unquestioning pride of place, the childlike belief that San Franciscans could do anything better than anybody else. *They called them the good old days because they were.*[22] [Emphasis added.]

Last, from a newspaper interview with bestselling author Irving Shulman on the occasion of the publication of his book *The Devil's Knee*:

We're most nostalgic, it seems, about the 50's—for some very good reasons. That was a time when wars were settled, there was a father figure in the White House, and countries were relatively at peace. We were busy making large families, and children were still considered a blessing. Prosperity was at hand and in the land. People were well mannered, crime was controlled, streets and neighborhoods safe, and the motor vehicle still seemed to be a safe animal to have around. Those days are light years away.[23]

What is most evident about these first-order nostalgia specimens, and thousands of others that could have as easily been culled, is the warm glow the speaker, despite occasional qualifications and asides, imparts to some past era: the celebration of now ostensibly lost values, the sense of some ineffable spirit of worth or goodness having escaped time, the conviction that, no matter how far advanced the present may be (and many are by no means prepared to

[22] *San Francisco Examiner and Sunday Chronicle*, August 12, 1973.

[23] Marilyn Tucker, "The Return of Shulman's Characters," *San Francisco Examiner and Sunday Chronicle*, April 22, 1973, *This World* section, p. 35.

concede any advance at all), it is in some deeper sense meaner and baser. The emotional posture is that of a yearning for return, albeit accompanied often by an ambivalent recognition that such is not possible. Later we shall have more to say on this yearning and its ambivalent reception by the self, particularly on how they influence the fashioning of our personal and collective histories.

Second Order or *Reflexive Nostalgia*: Here the person does more than sentimentalize some past and censure, if only implicitly, some present. In perhaps an inchoate though nevertheless psychologically active fashion he or she summons to feeling and thought certain empirically oriented questions concerning the truth, accuracy, completeness, or representativeness of the nostalgic claim. Was it really that way? If I were transported back to that time would things look to me as I now imagine they were then? Am I forgetting the bad and unpleasant things that occurred, and is this why it now seems to me to have been such a happy time? Indeed, deriving from the nostalgic mood a parallel set of questions is sometimes, though less frequently, directed at the present as well: Are things as bad as they seem? Looking back from some point in the future will I not feel as nostalgic for this period as I do now for that in the past? In addition, then, to the main interior nostalgic dialogue of virtuous past/unpleasant present, in Reflexive Nostalgia yet another voice is added: that of a Truth Squad or remonstrating Greek Chorus wanting to question, deflate, correct, and remind. The role is not unlike that of the Freudian ego, whose "reality testing" function consists in adjudicating the divergent claims of id and superego, except that here there is no *a priori* reason to assume (as perhaps there is not with the Freudian ego either) that its judgments are any more accurate or comprehensive than the claims of the nostalgic emotion *per se*. Again, some examples are in order. (But since Second Order elaborations of primary nostalgic reactions are usually so intertwined with each other, I have taken the liberty of italicizing those portions of the quotations that reveal the reflexive strain.)

From the interview with the young woman who romanticized her grandmother's era of tranquility and ease of travel:

> I think a lot of people feel that things have grown too crowded, complicated and fast-paced. That's why people now have such a tendency to look back. [Pause.] *But I don't know, maybe a hundred years ago people were saying the same thing then.* [Emphasis added.]

From an interview with another young woman who contemplates the apparent contradictions of remembered experience and historical judgment:

> You know, a lot of people nowadays are talking about "those good old nineteen thirties" *even though that's when we had a depression. Still that's also when my mother grew up and she has great memories from the thirties. So even though we know it was a pretty rotten era*—nobody had money, a lot of people were out of work—*if you talk to individuals who lived then many will tell you it was a beautiful time for them. So what you remember as good for you personally may not have been so good for the world.* [Emphasis added.]

From another Herb Caen column, appearing a few weeks after the one previously quoted, in which he pursues anew the elusive quest for the reality of the lost magic of the city's past:

> [What] WAS there about Old San Francisco that made it so special in the eyes of the world? Why did this small city, pulsating at continent's end under a cocoon of fog, capture and fire the imagination of sophisticates who had been everywhere. *If there was a real magic, where did it go or is it still in the air, and if it has vanished indeed, how responsible are we who came in the wake of the myth-makers?* [Emphasis added.] [24]

From an interview with a middle-aged woman, a collector of pre–World War II memorabilia and a flea market fan:

[24] *San Francisco Examiner and Sunday Chronicle*, September 23, 1973.

You know, there's a great thing on now for glass milk bottles, the old pop-neck bottles which are hard to find. Recently we were at a flea market and somebody there had a lot of them for sale. I wanted to buy some, just for something to have. *But my husband said, "Forget it, don't start that." And he reminded me how awful milk from those bottles tasted before we had good refrigeration. . . . We really did start laughing about that, the awful warm milk in that old pop-neck milk bottle left at the door by the milkman.* So I didn't buy any, although I already did have a few stashed away. *That just shows you. I remembered how nice it was to have the pop-neck bottle delivered at the door by the milkman, but forgot about how awful the milk tasted.* [Emphasis added.]

From one of the Andrews Sisters, Patty, commenting on the popularity of the hit nostalgic Broadway play *Over Here* (the sisters had enjoyed an immense popularity as a vocal group in the late thirties and early forties and came out of retirement specially in 1973 to appear in this show):

It's funny that we would do a nostalgia thing on the Second World War, which was a tragedy at that time. [Emphasis added.] [25]

From the septuagenarian author of *Nostalgia, U.S.A:*

And with this we come to the heart and core of what I've been trying to say, and what is within my powers to remember. *I have not tried to idealize the year 1900. That year had its imperfections.* Indeed, half of our contentment was not that we were contented but that we believed that what was wrong with 1900 would by degrees and without too much effort on our part go away. We never thought we would look back to 1900 with regret. . .because our faith in the deep goodness of the universe would [later come] no longer [to] exist. [Emphasis added.] [26]

These quotations, of course, are not of a piece, as regards either their originality or level of abstractness. The differences among them are proof that the mere presence of a questioning, factually oriented voice in the inward-turning

---

[25] *San Francisco Chronicle*, December 12, 1973, p. 61.
[26] R. L. Duffus, *Nostalgia, U.S.A., or, If You Don't Like the 1960's Why Don't You Go Back Where You Came From?* (New York: W. W. Norton, 1963), pp. 124–125.

nostalgic conversation in no way fixes the channel or the conclusion of the conversation. Any number of outcomes is possible. The Truth Squad or Greek Chorus may indeed serve as a corrective to the excessive romantic claims of the nostalgic impulse. Alternatively, it may be discounted as picayune or churlish, an ungracious denial of our deepest, hence most credible, feelings regarding the past. Or the utterances of the Chorus may be, as in some Greek tragedy, purely ritualistic, a kind of platitudinous presence whose occasional incantations are meant only to emphasize the passionate force of what has been fated from the outset. And these few options far from exhaust the dramaturgic possibilities of the nostalgic dialogue. Much, of course, depends on who is being nostalgic, when, with whom, and under what circumstances.

But what is important here for understanding the nostalgic experience *qua* experience is the activation, the bringing out of the wings, of this always immanent presence, not the weight it carries or the exact course of action in which it results. This, by itself, adds dimension to and enriches the simple nostalgic reaction, making of it in its reflexivity a more complex human activity that can better comprehend our selves and our pasts.

Third Order or *Interpreted Nostalgia:* This moves beyond issues of the historical accuracy or felicity of the nostalgic claim on the past and, even as the reaction unfolds, questions and, potentially at least, renders problematic the very reaction itself. It resembles in some respects, though certainly it is not as rigorous or as sustained, the epoché or formal bracketing operation of phenomenological analysis.[27] The actor here seeks in some fashion to objectify the nostalgia he feels. He directs at it (again with varying diligence and to varying degree) *analytically oriented* questions concerning its sources, typical character, significance, and psychological purpose. Why am I feeling nostalgic? What may this mean for my past, for my now? Is it that I am likely to feel nostalgia at certain

---

[27] See Alfred Schutz, "Some Leading Concepts of Phenomenology" in *Collected Papers, Volume I*, pp. 102–109.

times and places and not at others? If so, when and where? What uses does nostalgia serve for me? For others? For the times in which we live?

Here the analysis of the experience, however rudimentary, fleeting, or mistaken, comes in some part to be fused with the primary experience itself, causing it to become something more than a mere proclamation of, or even dialogue upon, past beauties and lost virtues. How *much* more will vary, to be sure, with persons and occasions: for the philosopher or psychologist accustomed to scrutinizing his inner states, perhaps a great deal more; for the man on the street immersed in the apparent certainties of what Schutz terms "the natural attitude,"[28] probably not nearly as much. In either case, what is important for this discussion is that the framing of the nostalgic response—this stepping outside, if only momentarily, of its givenness—adds yet another dimension to the experience and to its ability to illuminate our life situation.

In the quotations that follow I shall again italicize those segments which, however briefly or marginally, signify the cognitive shift to an interpretative perspective.

Again, Herb Caen, from the column quoted earlier where he reflects further on the nostalgia inspired elusive search for the magical beauty of San Francisco's past:

> You keep looking for the magic and now and then when the wind and the light are right, and the air smells ocean-clean, and a white ship is emerging from the Golden Gate mist into the Bay, and the towers are reflecting the sun's last rays—*at moments like that you turn to the ghosts and ask, "Was this the way it was?" And there is never an answer.* [Emphasis added.] [29]

From the eighteenth-century essayist James Beattie explaining why homesickness is felt more strongly for mountain settings:

> For precipices, rocks, and torrents are durable things; *and, being*

[28] *Ibid.*

[29] *San Francisco Examiner and Sunday Chronicle,* September 23, 1973.

more striking to the fancy than any natural appearances in the
plains take faster hold of the memory; and may therefore more frequently recur to the absent native, *accompanied with an idea of the*
pleasures formerly enjoyed in those places, and with regret that he
is now removed to so great a distance from them. [Emphasis added.] [30]

From Rousseau's *Confessions,* which while not about
nostalgia *per se* treats of a subject very close to it, namely,
those experiences that later give rise to pleasurable memory:

I have observed that, in the vicissitudes of a long life, *the periods*
of the sweetest enjoyments, and the liveliest pleasures, are not,
however, those whose rememberance most wins or touches me.
These short moments of delirium and passion, however lively they
may be, are no more, and that from their vivacity even, than very
distant points pricked on the line of life. *They are too rare and too*
rapid to constitute a state; and the happiness my heart regrets is not
composed of fugitive instants, but a simple and permanent state,
which has nothing violent in itself, but whose duration tempers the
charm to a degree of reaching, at last, supreme felicity. [Emphasis
added.] [31]

Last, from a cartoon by William Hamilton, the witty
and wry observer of the foibles of fashionalbe, upper-middle-
class cosmopolites. Shown are an almost matronly woman
and her prosperous-looking escort over cocktails in what
seems to be a supper club. The woman remarks: "What do
you suppose it means, Nedsy, when everything that's going
on consists of stuff that's coming back?"[32]

The Relationship of the Three Orders

Some points of clarification and qualification remain to be
made concerning the three orders of nostalgia and their
relationship to each other.

[30] Quoted in Christopher Salvesen, *The Landscape of Memory: A*
Study of Wordsworth's Poetry (Lincoln: University of Nebraska
Press, 1965), pp. 41–42.

[31] Quoted in *Ibid.*, p. 179.

[32] *The New Yorker,* March 25, 1974, p. 42.

To begin with, whereas it is probably true that in some crude quantitative sense (assuming it were possible somehow to collect statistics on the phenomenon) Simple Nostalgia is experienced more frequently than Reflexive, and Reflexive, in turn, more than Interpreted, this should not be taken to imply some invidious or pejorative relationship among them. From simple paeans of praise to the past to abstruse philosophical ratiocinations on man's encounter with time, each level—as much poetry, art, and even certain of the examples given above attest—is capable of its own vulgarizations, inanities, and illogic, just as each is capable of perspicacity, profundity, and elegance of statement. Thus, there is nothing necessarily "better" about the two higher orders of nostalgia, even if we allow that the Reflexive and Interpreted subsume, by definition, more complex cognitive perspectives than does the Simple. But at the same time their very complexity lends itself to a certain muddledness as well. Thus, there is the example of the author quoted earlier who seeks to "interpret" the current nostalgia vogue for the thirties by telling us what "really happened" then rather than what is going on now. Similarly, there is that puritanical brand of biographical censorship which in the wake of a Reflexive recognition that the past was actually different from the way Simple Nostalgia would have it, goes on to deny the legitimacy, and sometimes even the subjective reality, of nostalgic feeling *per se*. Such is usually the case with persons who are given to protesting that the only thing that matters to them is THE TRUTH; all other states of mind are to them suspect, if not actually illegitimate.

Second, it seems to be the case that once past childhood all of us, because we are reflective beings, are capable of experiencing and do experience all three levels of nostalgic reaction. I say this to dispel any implication of (odd as it may sound) a "nostalgia élite"—some specially chosen or self-designated cadre whose intuitions, sensibilities, and pronouncements regarding the allurements of the past are "purer," "more elevated," or "socially more productive" than the ostensibly baser subjectivities of their fellows. As a human emotion nostalgia, like love, hate, joy, and fear, is in all its simplicity and complexity "open" to all, even though persons will differ in their propensity to experience it. This, of course, is not to deny (although more on this later) that such social roles as age, sex, ethnicity, family status, and occupation and such phenomena as social and geographical mobility serve to structure differentially our relations to the past and, hence, to the nostalgic possibilities extant therein. But patterning, which surely there is, should not in and of itself be equated with the invidious ordering implied by the concept of "an élite."

Last, there is the danger that the differentiation of three orders of nostalgic experience will be taken to imply some necessary experiential progression from one to the other, usually from "lower" to "higher," or that the actor himself is consciously aware of these inner shifts of perspective. Neither suggestion is intended. The "orders" of nostalgic experience should be viewed as analytical categories and not as phenomena directly experienced by the subjects themselves, even if when we employ such categories we seek primarily to explain, that is, to translate into some set of understandable relationships, what it is the subject feels, thinks, and does.[33] For the subject himself, the experience is "of a piece" as he moves vividly from one "level" to another, as his mind leaps back and forth between them and as he

---

[33] For useful discussions of the analyst–subject category distinction see Sheldon D. Messinger et al., "Life as Theatre: Some Notes on the Dramaturgic Approach to Social Reality," Sociometry 25 (September 1962): 98–110, and Alfred Schutz, "Common Sense and Scientific Interpretations of Human Action" in Collected Papers, Volume I, pp. 41–47. Of course, in the social sciences, unlike the natural sciences, all analyst categories are potentially, through becoming known and accepted by the subjects, subject categories as well. To pursue this paradox further, however, would take us too far afield. See Fred Davis, "The Martian and the Convert: Ontological Polarities in Social Research," Urban Life and Culture 2, no. 3 (October 1973): 333–343.

breaks his train of thought and emotion only to soon return to it. There is no need for *him* to be conscious of these gyrations, to finely differentiate and to classify; and if perchance he chooses to, it is usually for reasons other than the scientific ones that concern us here. Indeed, as with the other human emotions, to become *too* conscious of the mechanism of nostalgia is to endanger the ability to experience it.

Conclusion

We have by now come far, I think, in the qualitative description of the nostalgic experience. Yet it must be allowed, alas, that its vivid essence still eludes us, irrespective of the words we choose or the context we set them in. Perhaps in the end its essence can only be grasped (other than via the experience itself) not in prose, but through some such medium as music, dance, or poetry and possibly through painting and some kinds of photography—in other words, via some symbolic medium which more directly engages our feelings without the intervening step of denotation or syntax. This is, to be sure, an instance of the familiar paradox that what can be evoked cannot in its truest sense be described and vice versa, that is, the classic contradiction of analysis and experience. Yet, in continuing the quest for a word that most nearly captures the "tone," the "feel," the "texture" of the subjective state of nostalgia one is, ironically, drawn closer and closer to the "diagnosis" made by Dr. Johannes Hofer some three centuries ago, to wit: homesickness, although here modified by an understanding that for moderns it is a homesickness severely stripped of connotations of geographic place and psychopathology. So amended, there is perhaps no word that better evokes the odd mix of present discontents, of yearning, of joy clouded with sadness, and of small paradises lost. That is, no word other than nostalgia itself.

MR. SAMMLER: *"I see you have these recollections."*
  WALLACE: *"Well, I need them. Everybody needs his
  memories. They keep the wolf of insignificance from
  the door."*

> Saul Bellow, Mr. Sammler's
> Planet *(New York: Viking,
> 1970)*

*The conviction of one's own past as a complete reposi-
tory of things that have happened, even though they
are now unknown, is nevertheless invincible and inexorable. And for good reason. Such conviction
represents the continuity of the self, which is an
indispensable aspect of experiencing oneself as an
integrated person, or "being normal." The sense of
a meaningful continuity is therefore as "true" as it
is necessary. We need the feeling of order and continuity so as to cope with the unending onslaught of
external and internal experiences. We therefore have
to impose our order on their flux and, if one cannot
grasp continuity, make it up in some fashion ourselves. The sureness of "I was" is a necessary component of the sureness of "I am."*

> Frederick Wyatt, "The
> Reconstruction of the
> Individual and of the Col-
> lective Past," in Robert W.
> White, ed., The Study of
> Lives *(New York: Ather-
> ton, 1963), p. 319*

2

NOSTALGIA AND IDENTITY

IF, AS I HAVE MAINTAINED, nostalgia is a distinctive way, though only one among several ways we have, of relating our past to our present and future, it follows that nostalgia (like long-term memory, like reminiscence, like daydreaming) is deeply implicated in the sense of who we are, what we are about, and (though possibly with much less inner clarity) whither we go. In short, nostalgia is one of the means—or, better, one of the more readily accessible psychological lenses—we employ in the never ending work of constructing, maintaining, and reconstructing our identities. To carry the optical metaphor a step further, it can be thought of as a kind of telephoto lens on life which, while it magnifies and prettifies some segments of our past, simultaneously blurs and grays other segments, typically those closer to us in time.

In this chapter, I wish to examine some of the general dimensions of nostalgic experience as they pertain to identity formation, maintenance, and reconstruction. I shall reserve for the next chapter a more focused appraisal of nostalgia's significance for effecting transitions among successive phases of the life career.

Continuity and Discontinuity of Identity

Of the tremendous range of concerns and issues subsumed by the concept "identity," one that obviously bears critically on the phenomenon of nostalgia is the question of the continuities and discontinuities we experience in our sense of self.[1] For the person the dilemma posed in this regard is, as for social organization generally, the classic one of effecting change while simultaneously ensuring a modicum of order and stability during the processes of change. Just as no organized entity, be it a person, a group, or some larger collectivity, can for long retain its integrity (and thus in some sense survive) in the face of too many changes occurring too rapidly in succession, so, at the other extreme, is survival threatened by the failure to adapt to either changed environmental conditions or altered internal demands. Indeed, it is by no means unusual for both external and internal demands to be activated simultaneously, thus making change that much more difficult and problematic. Moreover, so conscious are we of this dilemma, so often have scholars and scientists speculated upon it, that it can truly be said to form one of the dominant dialectics of Western thought, one whose arc of contention neatly calibrates much political doctrine, religious thought, general philosophy, scientific methodology, and, of course, humble opinion. Be that as it may, at the level at which we shall address the issue of continuity and discontinuity here—namely that of the person, his or her being,

[1] For some excellent general social psychological discussions of identity, see Anselm Strauss, *Mirrors and Masks: The Search for Identity* (Glencoe, Ill.: Free Press, 1959), and Erik H. Erikson, *Identity and the Life Cycle* (New York: International Universities Press, 1959).

self-image, and distinctive aura of lived separateness in the world—it is important to recognize that the complex amalgam of concept and sentience which we so inadequately refer to as "the self" is every bit as beset by the conflicting imperatives of change and stability as all other levels of organization with which social scientists deal, from the small group to the world order.

How, then, does nostalgia play into the continuing quest for personal identity, the attempt to salvage a self from the chaos of raw, unmediated experience? In the clash of continuities and discontinuities with which life confronts us, nostalgia clearly attends more to the pleas for continuity, to the comforts of sameness and to the consolations of piety, at least in the Pickwickian sense in which the term has been employed by Kenneth Burke.[2] Some of my informants, taking advantage of the interpretative possibilities the interview afforded them, seemed quite aware of this and all but said as much, as witness the observations of a man in his mid-twenties about to be divorced and about to start a new business venture. Speaking of how crucial the friendship circle of his late teens and early twenties had been for his nostalgic memory, he went on to state:

> I think the past can be a great standard and a great motivator too. I don't think it is a healthy thing to live in the past, to feel that it was best then and to remain there. But I do think it is a good comparison sometimes to see where you are going in terms of where you've been, to compare what your real goals and aims are with what you think you're going to get.

[2] I.e., remaining loyal to the sources of one's being. Kenneth Burke, *Permanence and Change* (Los Altos, Calif.: Hermes, 1954), pp. 71–74. From this perspective, nostalgia, at the individual level, is analogous to certain rituals at the group level that countermand what Turner has interestingly termed "structural amnesia," i.e., the convenient dropping from memory of past relations and obligations, a tendency he attributes to "mobile and fissile" societies of which our own is a good example. Victor W. Turner, *Schism and Continuity in an African Society* (Manchester, England: Manchester University Press, 1957), pp. 294–295.

The nostalgic reaction, then, can be said to be of a distinctly conservative bent, even if on occasion it has served radical ends as well.[3] If in its distaste for or alienation from the present it still envisions a better time, it is a time we have already known. It reassures us of past happiness and accomplishment and, since these still remain on deposit, as it were, in the bank of our memory, it simultaneously bestows upon us a certain current worth, however much present circumstances may obscure it or make it suspect. And current worth, as any bank loan officer will tell us, is entitled to some claim on the future as well.

This, perhaps, states the matter too sententiously. A more careful analysis of the "rhetoric" of nostalgia is necessary to gain an appreciation of how admirably the phenomenon furthers continuity of identity—or how, in the decimated imagery of a Saul Bellow character, "it manages to keep the wolf of insignificance from the door." But, before undertaking the analysis, two basic points deserve to be reiterated: (1) the nostalgic evocation of some past state of affairs always occurs in the context of present fears, discontents, anxieties, or uncertainties, even though they may not be in the forefront of awareness, and (2) it is these emotions and cognitive states that pose the threat of identity discontinuity (existentially, the panic fear of the "wolf of insignificance") that nostalgia seeks, by marshaling our psychological re-

---

[3] As, for example, with certain nativistic or revival movements in which the rejection of externally imposed identities is so profound as to inspire natives to translate their nostalgia for the folk past into revolutionary action. Or, as Frederic Jameson observes in his essay on the noted Marxist literary critic Walter Benjamin:

> But if nostalgia as a political motivation is most frequently associated with fascism, there is no reason why a nostalgia conscious of itself, a lucid and remorseless dissatisfaction with the present on the grounds of some remembered plenitude, cannot furnish as adequate a revolutionary stimulus as any other; the example of Benjamin is there to prove it.

Frederic Jameson, "Walter Benjamin, or Nostalgia," *Salmagundi*, no. 10-11 (Fall and Winter 1969-70), p. 68.

sources for continuity, to abort or, at the very least, deflect. This nostalgia-borne dialectic of the search ·for continuity amid threats of discontinuity (and the synthesis that can be effected between them) is nicely captured in the symbolism of an "old tweed coat" that one of my informants, a young artist, employed (earlier he had told me he was about to go abroad to study and was not at all sure whether he would find a good teacher there or whether the move would advance his career):

> You ask what nostalgia feels like to me? It feels like an old tweed coat. That stuff stays alive. It stays around, and the tweed coat I saw in the store yesterday is just like the ones I remember from when I was a kid. (Pause.) But I'm not going to go out and buy a tweed coat or cut my hair short again or get some button-down shirts and argyle socks like they wore in the fifties. Maybe I'll get the tweed coat, but I'll incorporate it into my current reality.

Continuity of Identity: Nostalgia's Cultivation of Appreciative Stances Toward Former Selves

To speak of "continuity of identity" is to imply something more than a disinterested and uneventful continuation through time of those images and apprehensions of self which we acquire in the course of growing up, i.e., those images and apprehensions which make it possible for our *now* selves to recognize, know, and feel some sympathetic bond with, earlier selves that are temporally no longer accessible to us. With those for whom changing circumstance is constantly posing the question "Who am I?"—and in the modern world this includes many for much of the time—the mere retrieval of biographical facts from our pasts (date and place of birth, nationality, childhood diseases, school grades, and the like) is not enough to ensure continuity of identity. Some evaluative or appreciative stance toward former selves is required as well. And, whereas the question "Who am I?"—which perforce must be answered largely in terms of "Who

35

was I?"—does not invariably evoke a favorable response from the self (some fall victim to depression, others commit suicide), the human proclivity to respond positively to this question is perhaps as universal as it is familiar. In short, people want to think well of themselves.

Note that I have said *well*, not gloriously, brilliantly, famously, or any of the other heroic superlatives by which a few choose to measure their being, but which most of us find extravagant, unattainable, or, more simply, compromised by the, at best, "only fair" bargains that life has dealt us. But to think *well* of oneself, however variably this has been defined at different times and in different places, is a standard that society not only permits but practically enjoins. Indeed, some social philosophers have gone so far as to argue that the quintessence of social order resides in the institutional capacity to arrange affairs in such a manner as to encourage the vast majority of persons to think "well" of themselves most of the time. To allow for less is to sow the seeds of mass disaffection, if not actually to usher in the Hobbesian specter of the war of all against all.

This is the aspect of identity continuity, as meaningful emotionally for the person as it is socially necessary, that nostalgia attends to so nicely. However simply or complexly, crudely or subtly, it is of the essence of nostalgic experience to cultivate appreciative stances to former selves. In so doing, it can make the present seem less frightening and more assimilable than it would otherwise appear. (Of course, to make it *seem* so is not to make it *actually* so; consideration of the ways that the *appearance* of a benign reality can promote or inhibit its realization lies, however, well beyond the aims of this work.) The rhetorical formula seems simple enough: if, as my nostalgic evocation of the past tells me, I was lovable and worthy then despite adverse or dangerous conditions, I am likely to prove lovable and worthy now despite the anxieties and uncertainties of the present. To fail persistently at forging this restitutive link between a past and a present self is quite possibly to expose one's being to that terrifying "hell of timelessness" which the psychiatrist Meerloo sees as characteristic of schizophrenics.

[So] many beginning schizophrenics complain about this lack of awareness of continuity. In their personal universe of time they experience a sudden emptiness, a being alone in eternity. They are caught by the great urge to undo time, to rise beyond fate and death and causality. The various historical developments are not experienced as coordinated, time does not flow any more. This is their subjective way of announcing a withdrawal from reality. The schizophrenic catastrophe—the experience of breakdown of inner structure—is often explained by them as a downfall of the outer world, as aimlessness of existence and as the hell of timelessness. Timelessness here means: no future.[4]

Continuity of Identity:
Nostalgia's Muting of the Negative

The proclivity to cultivate appreciative attitudes toward former selves is closely related to nostalgia's earlier-noted tendency to eliminate from memory or, at minimum, severely to mute the unpleasant, the unhappy, the abrasive, and, most of all, those lurking shadows of former selves about which we feel shame, guilt, or humiliation. (Not, of course, that these grim residues are eliminated from memory *as such,* but rather from the nostalgic reconstruction thereof. Or, as one wit aptly put it, "Nostalgia is memory with the pain removed.")[5] This insight into nostalgia's ability to filter out the unpleasant was so widespread among my informants that it served as a springboard for them to ascend to those higher orders of nostalgic experience which in the last chap-

[4] Joost A. M. Meerloo, "The Time Sense in Psychiatry," in J. T. Fraser, ed., *The Voices of Time* (New York: Braziller, 1966), p. 246.
[5] Quoted in Herb Caen's column, *San Francisco Chronicle*, April 15, 1975.

ter I termed the Reflexive and the Interpretive. A young woman, for example, allows that nearly all of her nostalgic memories derive from her adolescence and not her childhood:

> Except for those Saturday afternoon shopping trips downtown with my grandma when she would treat me to lunch at a big department store, I've blocked out a lot of my childhood. (Slightly nervous laugh.). I don't think I was that happy as a child, and that's perhaps why. Whereas I think that during adolescence although I was unhappy a lot, it was good unhappiness, if that makes any sense.

Indeed, so carried away can the nostalgic mood make one that he or she obliterates from memory the unmistakable pain and tragedy associated with what has been singled out for adoration. Again that wry observer of the contemporary nostalgia syndrome, the cartoonist William Hamilton, has registered what is probably the final word on the matter. Three late-middle-aged "boardroom" types are seated around drinks in what appears to be the bar of a private club; one remarks "THE Depression, THE Game in the Bowl, THE War. Damn it, ours was THE life!"[6]

But even where adversity and anguish are known not to have been present, nostalgia still retains the capacity to impart charm and goodness to what at the time may have been experienced as ordinary and uneventful. With characteristic felicity and insight another humorist, Russell Baker, nicely captures this tendency and the mechanism of its manifestation. Writing on the disquieting exposure of the awkward, the unattractive, and the anachronistic as revealed in rediscovered family photographs long since put away and shielded from memory, Baker goes on to observe:

> [Most] of us, when we get behind the camera, are doomed to be embalmers. What we can do, however, is take great pictures in our heads, and not only take them, but store them so that they improve with the years. We can add color, movement, emotion, feel, taste,

[6] *San Francisco Examiner and Chronicle,* Sunday *Punch,* April 21, 1974.

sound and even smell. What's more, as the years go by we can, and usually do, edit and improve them. I have one of these (mental) snapshots taken years ago by some hollyhocks in my grandmother's yard. Not only does it show the pink of the flowers, in tints at least as lovely as they were on that distant summer day, but it also contains the incredible blue of the sky—sometimes the sky is filled with glistening cumulus clouds, other times it is the purest blue— as well as the hum of a bumblebee, the distant rumble of a thresh- ing machine, the smell of wild roses on the fence . . . and, behind me, for this camera can also photograph through 360 degrees, the great house. This is a splendid snapshot. Am I to believe that this is the way it really was, or should I accept this more recent camera version which tried to tell me that my grandmother's house was only a small gray dilapidation and her front yard a small plot over- grown with weeds?[7]

But the point is not merely nostalgia's facility for "muting the negative," as it were. Rather, it is that in so doing nos- talgia furthers the purposes of continuity of identity by reassuring the now self that it is "as it was then": deserving, qualified, and fully capable of surmounting the fears and uncertainties that lie ahead.

Continuity of Identity: The Dialogue of Rediscovering a Secret Self

Growing out of his fascination with the subtle dialectic of individualizing and socializing tendencies in group life, Simmel long ago commented on, as have Riesman and Goffman[8] more recently from different vantage points, the recurrent tendency of the person stubbornly to preserve a

---

[7] Russell Baker, "The Snapshots in My Own Mind," *San Francisco Sunday Examiner and Chronicle*, Editorial section, July 21, 1975.

[8] Kurt H. Wolff, *The Sociology of Georg Simmel* (Glencoe, Ill.: Free Press, 1950), pp. 26–39; David Riesman, "The Ethics of We Happy Few," in *Individualism Reconsidered* (Glencoe, Ill.: Free Press, 1954), pp. 39–54; and Erving Goffman, "Role Distance," in *Ecounters* (Indianapolis: Bobbs-Merrill, 1961), pp. 85–152.

portion of the self from the ascriptions, expectations, and imputations that others direct at him or her by virtue of his or her apparent social identity. The quality of selfhood all these authors have sought to analyze is that of the still, small voice within us, which, secretly at least, is forever qualifying, denying, and upsetting the formulae by which "the powers that be" seek to comprehend and regulate our behavior. "You think I'm serene; I'm really a cauldron of seething passions." "Don't think because I'm a bank president I'm stuffy; my collar is loose, my feet are on the desk and there's a THIMK poster on the wall behind me." "I was the most popular girl in my high school class. Everyone thought me tremendously self-assured and sexy when in fact I was terrified of being found out for the insecure and unattractive person I really felt myself to be." And so forth. We are all familiar with the scenario; the studied anomaly, the cultivated eccentricity, the intimate confession, the whispered revelation which seeks to convince the self and sometimes the world at large that we are not (or at least not quite) our jobs, our social roles, our conventionalized appearances; that "beneath it all" we are something more intriguing, more sensitive, more complex, more daring. In short, that we are not like "all the others."

Now, nostalgic recall evinces a strong partiality for this genre of *amour propre*. As the colloquial French expression "nostalgie pour la boue" (the mud) hints at but does not quite convey, it likes to fasten on those periods in our past when we thought and felt ourselves different; when we espoused minority tastes in movies, music, comics, clothes, and ice cream flavors; when our secret sorrows and exclusion from the mainstream seemed somehow more enobling than the "vulgar enjoyments" of the crowd. Why should this be the case, especially since, as we shall see later, so many of the other faces of nostalgia search for, build upon, and memorialize what we hold in common with others, those shared experiences of an earlier time that symbolize what was and is, after all, *our* era and *our* generation?

Again, the answer seems to lie not so much with what actually may have been unique in our pasts as it has to do with nostalgia's abiding involvement with the existential problem of sustaining continuity of identity in the face of new demands, with assimilating the inevitable alterations in relationships occasioned by our destined passage through the life cycle, and, more diffusely, with calming the disquietude aroused by almost any alteration in one or another of our many statuses, particularly with those occupational and familial roles that are deeply implicated in our core concept of self. In sum, all those "events" that bestir our sense of aloneness in the world, our feelings of estrangement from others and, perhaps, disaffection from life.

Nostalgia's penchant for prizing "strange" and private facets of a past self bears an interesting isomorphic relationship to current life situations that are problematic for our identity. It is this isomorphism which more than anything explains the favored place accorded such memories and the poignant feelings they evoke in us. It is as if by harking back to those (probably recast) times of sweet strangeness, we assure ourselves that, just as we then felt odd, different, alone, and estranged, and yet managed somehow to emerge from it all intact and possibly even enhanced, so shall we again. The formula is almost ideal: at one at the same time we quiet our fears of the abyss while bestowing an endearing luster on past selves that may not have seemed all that lustrous at the time.

Still other balms and consolations are afforded by nostalgia's propensity to fasten on what was offbeat, marginal, odd, different, secret, and privatized about our former selves. Two in particular are worth mentioning. First there is the matter of personal vindication, petty though its objects may be. Since in the contemporary world so many of the minority (and even *avant garde*) tastes and involvements of yesterday quickly become, via the acceleration afforded them through the mass media, the dominant modes of today, it is by no means uncommon to awaken to the recognition that the

music, clothes, speech, and attitudes that uniquely symbol-
ized you and your small coterie last year have in the interim
come to symbolize a whole class or generation (an instance of
yesterday's cultivated nonconformity emerging as today's
acclaimed conformity, a phenomenon astutely analyzed by
Sapir in his classic essay on "Fashion").[9] As we shall detail
more fully in a later chapter, this phenomenon has, in recent
decades especially, become part and parcel of the experience
of "growing up" for whole cohorts of youth; hence, its
saliency for the developmental transition from late adolescence to early adulthood, a period that in other respects as
well is, as we shall also see, peculiarly vulnerable to nostalgic
exploitation. A recent newspaper report of a free Central
Park concert by the rock band Jefferson Starship (the Jefferson Airplane of the late nineteen-sixties) nicely depicts this
familiar yet slightly skewed and enigmatic phenomenon of
modern life:

> Rambling outdoor concerts like this used to be occasions that far
> transcended the music played at them. They were symbolic cluster-
> ings of a new society, laboratories for the way people would get
> along in the future. They were charged with purpose of one sort or
> another—political utopianism, hippie love vibes, religious release.
> But most everybody in high school looks like a hippie these days;
> the emblems of a counterculture have become the fashions of the
> mainstream. What used to be a challenging vanguard, posing musical
> and political alternatives, has become the establishment entertain-
> ment of the day.[10]

In any case—and despite the grossness and adulteration that
frequently mark the migration of taste from those few "in
the know" to the mass audience—the knowledge (indexed
and celebrated by innumerable taste coteries, little maga-
zines, underground publications, and feature writers) that
what you saw and felt then later became what was seen and

[9] Edward Sapir, "Fashion," in *Encyclopedia of the Social Sciences*,
Vol. VI (New York: Macmillan, 1931), pp. 139–144.

[10] John Rockwell, "Starship Concert in Park Stirs Nostalgia for Lost
Era," *New York Times*, May 13, 1975.

felt by "nearly everybody" is flattering to the self. It gives testimony to one's prescience, to a heightened sensitivity and oneness with the deepest impulses of an age. What better material for nostalgia's cultivation of an appreciative stance toward the self?

But it is not purely in its solitary, intrapsychic form that nostalgia's affinity for private and eccentric facets of former selves affords us comfort. This is because there is about the private—indeed, about its requirement to be ultimately recognized as such—a persistent, if muted, yearning to be made public. Hence the desire reported by many of my informants to share their nostalgic musings on secret selves and odd tastes (their own *petites madeleines* in their own Combrays) with others, sometimes friends but more often about-to-become friends inasmuch as this kind of sharing, this cautious mutual discovery of unexpected likenesses, is in and of itself the very elixir of friend-making.[11] What we witness in this kind of nostalgic memory exchange is, of course, the wonderment of the revelation of how much more alike than different our "secret" pasts are: that you were not alone in fantasizing being a Chinese in a silk brocade gown; that at age ten upon going to bed the other too had play-acted chapters from an interminable adventure serial; that, amazingly, both of you had peered to the point of squinting at the cereal box which pictured a mother holding the very same cereal box whose picture pictured the same mother holding the same cereal box *ad infinitum* in paradoxical regress.

At one and the same time, then, our nostalgia for those aspects of our past selves that were "odd and different" becomes the basis for deepening our sentimental ties to others and for reassuring us that we are not *that* strange after all. Others, it turns out, were equally "strange." Secondly, therefore, it can be said that in this guise nostalgic

[11] See Murray S. Davis, *Intimate Realtions* (New York: Free Press, 1973), pp. 103–115.

sharing enhances the sense of our own normalcy, something which adolescents and young adults stand in special need of, given the social dislocations and identity strains to which they are subject. As a young woman I interviewed reported:

> It's more fun when you're sharing your nostalgic feelings and memories. You start talking with someone else, they'll come up with some memory from the time they were a kid, and you laugh and say "Oh, no! I had the same experience." And you're in awe that it's so much the same thing. You create this warm feeling between you, even though most people don't like to admit straight out that they're nostalgic.

Moreover, this assurance is conveyed in the context of an exchange that, by virtue of its intimacy, stops short of depriving us of that sense of uniqueness which initially clothed the nostalgic impulse.

The dialectic, then, is analagous in form to that structured by fashion: we are encouraged to be "different" but not so different as to seem freakish or unduly rebellious.[12] The contrast, of course, resides in the fact that fashion, much as it may draw on materials from the past, boldly announces itself as future-oriented, whereas nostalgia, much as it is burdened by future concerns, only surreptitiously alludes to them. But that the two are closely, perhaps inextricably tied is made evident by the frequency with which fashion exploits our nostalgic attachment to past styles and sensibilities[13]

Continuity of Identity:
The Erection of Benchmarks

Thus far I have spoken of how nostalgia serves the purposes of continuity of identity by (1) cultivating appreciative stances toward former selves, (2) screening from memory

[12] Sapir, "Fashion."
[13] See the especially astute observations of the *New Yorker* fashion writer Kennedy Fraser along these lines, quoted in Chapter 4, at note 19.

the unpleasant and shameful, and (3) rediscovering and, through a normalizing process, rehabilitating marginal, fugitive, and eccentric facets of earlier selves. Permeating all these dimensions, yet constituting an analytically separable element in the rhetoric of nostalgia is its powerful bench-marking potential—its capacity to locate in memory an earlier version of self with which to measure to advantage some current condition of the self. Typically the effect is that of leading the nostalgizer to infer, or perhaps distantly to intuit, some such self-appraisal as "Look how far I've come." This is in large part accomplished, of course, by nostalgia's notorious tendency to simplify and romanticize the past, so much so as to allow us to adopt an almost patronizing attitude to the "dear, sweet, simple, but alas now dead days of yore.[14] In reaching this conclusion we are also tacitly encouraged in the conviction that we have in the interim "grown" and "matured" and are now better equipped to confront the considerably more challenging demands of the present. Hence, in what perhaps qualifies as a marvel of rational condensation, nostalgia manages at one and the same time to celebrate the past, to diminish it, and to transmute it into a means for engaging the present. This inner dialogue wherein past virtues and simplicities encounter present challenges and complexities to make for a rich nostalgic stew is nicely illustrated in the following excerpt by a woman in her mid-twenties who in the course of the interview divulged that she was having great difficulty deciding whether she wanted to marry or pursue a career:

> I remember at Christmas time my friend Sharon came to the house for dinner and a number of other people were there too. We just started talking about growing up in the city. Sharon and I had, but no one else present did. And so, to play sort of a dirty trick on Sharon, I pulled out these letters she passed to me in high school

[14] Cf. Edward W. Rosenheim, Jr., "Nostalgia," *A Humanities Occasional Paper* presented at a Visiting Committee to the Division of the Humanities, December 19, 1974, The University of Chicago, 1975.

during class breaks. They're letters that I wouldn't throw away for anything. So I let the other people read these letters of Sharon at age sixteen. They were really very funny, very amusing letters and we were all laughing over them and talking about how easy life was then. Although at the time it didn't seem to be very easy. You know, our major concern was going to the dance on Friday night and what we were going to wear. And we were laughing about how nice it was. . .but I only realize that in retrospect, because at the time it was very complicated for me. Although now that I look back on it I realize that it wasn't half as complicated as my life is now. I was a lot freer then I think. My major concerns were social things, who my date was and who Sharon's was. That's all that Sharon's letters had to do with. . . That was the center of all of our problems. It seemed complex and difficult then, but as I look back on it now it seems as if it was all so much lighter.

To the degree that nostalgia's talent for inferring to implicit advantage a present self from a retrojection of some past self may seem to contradict nostalgia's underlying proclamation of the superiority of things past, it should be noted that this "distortion" of the modality becomes possible only as the emotion evolves beyond its simple form toward what in the preceding chapter I termed Second Order or Reflexive Nostalgia. That is, the actor, much like my informant above, must be able to question the "reality" of the nostalgic claim vis-à-vis his or her current life situation. And, however uninformed or inaccurate this assessment may be, some conscious comparative perspective toward the self must be adopted if the person is to come away from the nostalgic exercise reassured in his or her ability to cope competently with the present.

The Authenticity of the Nostalgic Emotion

In this discussion of nostalgia's role in the furtherence of continuity of identity, questions are likely to arise concerning the historical truthfulness and psychological authenticity of nostalgia's images, claims, and conclusions. Clearly it is an emotion that plays tricks on us. No matter how suspicious of it we are, it still will continue to simplify, sentimentalize, prettify, and otherwise distort our pasts. In deference then to the quest for some higher standard of personal truth, is the emotion to be denounced, checked, ridiculed, or perhaps even forbidden? A rhetorical question to be sure, but one which, oddly enough, preoccupies some persons, groups, and sects sufficiently to cause them to issue warnings and denunciations concerning nostalgia's legitimacy and worth. Some even go so far as to suggest that the world would be a better place if only nostalgia could be expunged from the repertoire of human emotions.

I shall have more to say later on the political-ideological opposition to nostalgia. For now, though, to the degree that nostalgia, like rain or remorse, may require defense, it should be pointed out that, unlike other emotions or forms of consciousness to which the human is heir, nostalgia functions under the constitution and constraints of a *lived* past. Lacking the imaginative abandon of fantasy or the caprice of dreaming, nostalgia at least purports to represent the true places, events, and moods of our past, even if our powers of historical reflection may cause us to question whether "it was indeed that way." Such warranted suspicions aside, nostalgia aims—more often inaccurately to be sure—to grasp the essence of "the way things really were." In this resides the virtue and pathos of nostalgia: it can only draw from the meager materials of one's *own past* existence; unlike "bolder" emotions and mental states, it cannot fabricate out of whole cloth the person, the scene, or the event that never was.

Thus in some ultimate sense nostalgia retains the accent, if not the verisimilitude, of past reality; and, to the degree that we suspect its verisimilitude, which we often do, we are left to search in our minds for that reality. Not, of course, that we finally arrive at THE TRUTH of our pasts, but rather that the search itself is edifying and humanizing inasmuch as it affords us the imaginative means for better reconciling past being with present circumstance.

The constraint of a lived past on nostalgia and nostalgia's inability knowingly and recklessly to obliterate it (or to fabricate another past in its place) is charmingly illustrated in an informant's report on what she is able to discard and not discard from her "memory box." This is a large cardboard box in which she has saved from childhood and adolescence such memorabilia as matchbook covers from restaurants she had been taken to by boyfriends, cubes of sugar from the high school prom, picnic spoons, theater programs, and so forth—along with, of course, much intimate material like diaries, love poems of her own composition, notes, letters, and other confessional missives from former boyfriends and girlfriends. In a fit of nostalgia she would periodically return to the memory box, go through it, and rearrange its contents, bringing some things to the fore and relegating others to obscure places, adding more recently acquired keepsakes, and discarding others that no longer seemed particularly vivid or meaningful. (It is as if with each such rearrangement she, in an almost literal sense, designed a slightly different past for herself.) The obvious question suggests itself: what did she discard, what did she keep? Typically, she found herself throwing out such small artifacts as the prom sugar cubes, picnic spoons, matchbook covers, and the like. The diaries, poems, class notes, letters, and other missives were never discarded, even though on rereading them she invariably found them vapid and terribly embarrassing. Why, if they were so embarrassing and compromising of her current image of self, did she not discard them as she had the sugar cubes and matchbook covers? This, she allowed, she could never bring herself to do since it somehow seemed "unfair and wrong" to treat so cavalierly of one's former self, no matter how jejune or gawkish it now seemed to her. "Maybe I'll move the notes and letters to a far corner of the box, but throw them out? Never!"

Conclusion

It should by now be evident: nostalgia thrives on transition, on the subjective discontinuities that engender our yearning for continuity.[15] It is because of this, as we shall see in the next chapter, that the nostalgic reaction is most pronounced at those transitional phases in the life cycle that exact from us the greatest demands for identity change and adaptation—for example, that from childhood to pubescence, from adolescent dependency to adult independence, from single to married, from mate to parent, from parent to in-law, from worker to retiree, from spouse to widowed. Similarly, in its collective manifestations nostalgia also thrives, as we shall see in a still later chapter, on the rude transitions rendered by history, on the discontinuities and dislocations wrought by such phenomena as war, depression, civil disturbance, and cataclysmic natural disasters—in short, those events that cause masses of people to feel uneasy and to wonder whether the world and their being are quite what they always took them to be.

But the relationship of identity discontinuity to the nostalgic reaction is neither perfect nor continuous. Just as it is almost impossible to conceive of nostalgia in a world of perfect, unrelieved continuity, that is, a world without transition, so is it equally difficult to conceive of it in a world of ceaseless discontinuity. Inasmuch as the feeling of discontinuity must finally find its existential base, as it were, in some earlier apprehension of continuity, those discontinuities which in their onrush prove too prolonged, disparate, or unassimilable would in short order deprive nostalgia of the homey, warmly remembered material it requires to play the beguiling game of celebrating the past so as to better endure

[15] See Charles A. A. Zwingmann, "'Heimweh' or 'Nostalgic Reaction': A Conceptual Analysis and Interpretation of a Medico-Psychological Phenomenon," unpublished Ph.D. dissertation, School of Education, Stanford University, 1959, p. 199.

the future. Discontinuities of too great a magnitude can only give rise to chaos or psychosis; and it is precisely these states that nostalgia in its sometimes charming, sometimes pathetic way aims to arm us against.

Nostalgia, then, is fashioned from the alternating continuities and discontinuities of our lives and times. It requires both, though probably more of the latter, if only to set the process in motion. Or, as that penetrating writer on the American penchant for nostalgic indulgence, Russell Baker, has rendered the formula: "Asian villagers living for generations in one place would be baffled by nostalgia. It is an affliction of traveling races who do not like where they have arrived and have no taste for the next destination.[16]

---

[16] Russell Baker, "Past Shock," *New York Times Magazine*, Sunday, May 4, 1975, p. 6.

*But now I see that the extraordinary was in my own
vision. . . . I see my life in Paris with the added elements of fiction: lighting, focus, the gold patina
which memory adds to it, and they appear to me
more vividly, more separated from the quotidian
details which dilute it, from the unformed, the
excrescences, the dust or dullness of familiarity.
They are highlighted in this case by poignant memory
and a desire to relive it all, now that it is forever lost.*

> *Anaïs Nin,* The Diary, *Vol. 6
> (New York: Harcourt Brace
> Jovanivich, 1976), p. 161*

*All experience has a historical character, but the error
is to treat the past in mechanical terms. The past,
rather, is the domain of contingency in which we accept events and from which we select events in order
to fulfill our potentialities and to gain satisfactions
and security in the immediate future. . . . Alfred
Adler used to point out that memory was a creative
process, that what we remember has significance for
our "style of life," and that the whole "form" of
memory is therefore a mirror of the individual's
style of life. What an individual seeks* to become de-
termines what he remembers of his *has been.*

> *Rollo May,* Existence *(New
> York: Basic Books, 1958),
> p. 69*

3

NOSTALGIA
AND
THE LIFE CYCLE

MORE PERHAPS THAN ANY OTHER concept in the cultural sciences, that of the life cycle affords us a bridge from the apparently intensely private quality of nostalgic experience to its sources in society and its consequences for collective life. For, while our movement from one stage of life to the next cannot but be "intensely personal," it is at the same time truly social in the deepest sense. On the personal side it is after all *we* who experience these changes and, from the ultimately irreducible subjectivity of our experience, we alone. Yet these movements, these changes and alterations, arrivals and departures, are not for the most part purely fortuitous or random in their occurrence. While certainly not fixed, inevitable, or dictated by society or culture in any gross deterministic sense, their timing, social substance, and trajectory are nonetheless structured or at least outlined by the values, expectations, common practices, and institutional arrangements of the social order in which they occur. And for those of us who, in Schutz's terms, happen to be *con-*

temporaries and *consociates*, these movements and fluctuations along the biographical time track are also marked, and often channeled as well, by the unique historic events, personalities, and occurrences of "our time," thereby serving further to collectivize the essential individuality of our biographies.[1]

Thus, our life careers acquire form, commonality, and comparability by virtue of the circumstance that we *typically* go to work in late adolescence or early adulthood, *typically* marry within a certain age span with mates *typically* from only certain age and sex categories, that we *typically* rear children during our middle years, and that we *typically* retire from work sometime in our sixties. It is, of course, of such cognitive and institutional materials that the life cycle, sociologically speaking, is made. Yet, on its subjective side it must be recognized that how these materials are used, how they are aligned, integrated, disentangled, or eluded over the life cycle will vary markedly among people, especially modern people for whom change, movement, and variability have in and of themselves come to be a dominant motif in the very design of life. (The apocryphal Frenchman notwithstanding, plus ca change, plus ce n'est pas la même chose.) Regarding the life passage then, it is as if its major destinations were plotted in advance save for our being given some freedom in choosing the manner and time of our arrival. And if perchance we are to bypass some destinations altogether (e.g., finding employment, marrying, bearing children), then we need "good" explanations for why we deviated from the "normal" itinerary.

It is to a consideration of these destinations and our more or less scheduled passage among them that we turn in this chapter for additional insight into the sources, nature, and consequences of nostalgic experience. For if as I stated in the previous chapter nostalgia thrives on the subjective appre-

[1] Alfred Schutz, *Collected Papers, Volume I* (The Hague: Martinus Nijhoff, 1962) pp. 15-19.

hension of transition, then what more fertile terrain for its flowering than the life cycle—that mock-up of our future being and becoming handed us at birth, which both shapes us and is to varying degrees shaped by us in the course of our traversing it? Yet these life cycle itineraries are, as I have suggested, infinitely more varied and complex in their historical, cultural, social, and characterological dimensions than could possibly be comprehended by any single scheme.[2] It is for this reason, not to mention the sheer dearth of research on how nostalgia and other forms of retrospective memory relate to the life cycle, that we are reduced here to a modest rather than exhaustive exploration of the relationship. That is, we shall look only at how nostalgia relates to sex role differentiation and how it relates to the transition from adolescence to adulthood and the transition from late adulthood to old age. And, even within this reduced frame, the discussion is further narrowed by its almost exclusive reliance on materials from contemporary American society. But since comprehensiveness as such is not our aim, perhaps even this shrunken and frayed account will be sufficient to suggest the multiple and important purposes served by nostalgia in effecting movement through the life cycle.

Sex Role and Nostalgia

Clearly, whether one is born male or female has been— at least until very recently, and arguably still is—the single most important attribute influencing the existential shape

[2] Mere mention of a few of the more obvious variations is perhaps sufficient to suggest the impossibility of the task: for example, societies in which the adolescent passage is sharply etched as against those in which it is barely noted; societies that revere elders in contrast to those which neglect or scorn them; societies with strictly segregated sex roles as against those with a much looser and interchangeable sexual division of labor; societies with a largely hereditary occupational system as against those with a free and open labor

and content of one's life career. There may then be some value in posing the simple-minded question:—who are the more nostalgic, men or women? Early studies, including the many by American psychologists during the 1930-1960 heyday of the "personality inventory" approach to behavioral phenomena, seemed to establish, though by no means conclusively, that men are the more nostalgic.[3]

This, of course, flies in the face of that familiar strain in popular thought which holds that women are the more sentimental, more romantic, more open to emotional influence, and in general more "feelings-oriented" and hence, one would infer, more nostalgia-prone. Yet, to the extent that the research finding does have some general validity we should not be surprised by it, given what has already been noted concerning nostalgia's source in the threat of identity discontinuity. Much anthropological research of a psychocultural bent has long maintained, after all, that in America, as in Western society generally, it is the male who experiences the sharper transitional discontinuities of status, role, and often geographical location as well.[4] The fixing of a sexual identity, the choice of occupation and attainment of a secure place therein, military service, the assumption of husband and father roles, unemployment and other breaks in the work career, and, finally, retirement and old age—these all seem to add up to a more disruptive and discontinuous

---

market; caste-bound societies vs. class or classless societies; monolithic and hierarchically organized societies vs. decentralized and more pluralistically based ones; and so forth. Needless to say, all of these variables (and others besides) have a profound effect on the chronological geometry and rhythms of the life cycle and on the subjective sense of continuity, transition, and discontinuity that accompanies it.

[3] Charles A. A. Zwingmann, "'Heimweh' or 'Nostalgic Reaction': A Conceptual Analysis and Interpretation of a Medico-Psychological Phenomenon," unpublished Ph.D. dissertation, School of Education, Stanford University, 1959, p. 151.

[4] The classic statement of the position is that of Ruth Benedict, "Continuities and Discontinuities in Cultural Conditioning," *Psychiatry* 1 (1938), 161-167.

life passage than do the equivalent and complementary status transitions in the woman's life cycle. Cultural anthropologists are inclined to explain the difference by pointing out that traditionally women's status passages occur in the familiar and reassuring context of home, family, and kin, whereas those of men are more likely to involve abrupt shifts of locale, reference group, life style and interpersonal atmospheres. "That Old Gang o' Mine" is, after all, a song of *male* barbershop quartets; it is hard to think of its nostalgic equivalent among women.

We can of course wonder whether, with the marked redefinitions of gender and sex roles currently under way in American society, women will not in time show themselves as nostalgis-prone as men. As women's freedom of choice expands, as the cultural expectations directed at them become less insular, parochial, and stereotyped, they too may find it necessary to enshroud their past selves nostalgically against the fears and uncertainties of prospective identities. Even now a simple research inquiry that might throw light on the question would be to determine whether mature "women in the world" (e.g., professional women, those in public life, and others who have wandered far from home, so to speak) experience nostalgia more often and more deeply than do their more homebound sisters. In a related fashion we can speculate that the nostalgic sentimentality sometimes attributed to the maiden aunt who "went to work because she never married" attests, perhaps, to an atypical role discontinuity in the lives of some women that is more commonly found in the lives of men.

Nostalgia and the Transition from Adolescence

While the nostalgic reaction can feed on any *prior* period in life, in Western society it is adolescence, and for the privileged classes early adulthood as well, that affords nostalgia its most sumptuous banquets. The reasons are in accord with much that has been said thus far. Basically, there is the circumstance that (for men in particular) few of life's transitions are as difficult, as strongly contrasted, as prolonged and replete with fateful uncertainties as that from adolescence to adulthood. Whether it be a matter of starting work, going off to college, performing military service, getting married, becoming a parent, or simply leaving home—typically it is a stressful combination of several of these—the essential psychosocial transition involves being carried in relatively short order from familiar places and persons to settings that are new, unfamiliar, and thus problematic in crucial respects. Not infrequently the change is so marked or abrupt (e.g., the sheltered youth being inducted into the army, the young girl who marries, starts a family, and sets up house hundreds of miles from her parental home) as to make it appear utterly alien and unassimilable. From a subjective standpoint then, the transition from social adolescence to adulthood is especially dramatic and well marked. This, in turn, accounts for its etching a sharp figure–ground contrast in one's life space. And given certain other conditions, the chief one being that the existential substance of the transition not be *so* disjunctive or *so* abrupt as to demolish prior identities altogether, it is, as Beardsley Ruml noted many years ago, precisely such strongly contrasting figure–ground identity configurations that are most conducive to nostalgic reactions.[5]

Some glancing sense of what is involved is conveyed in the interview observations of a young woman in her mid-twenties:

A friend was over the other evening and we got to talking about people I hadn't seen for awhile who seem to be going through experiences similar to what I'm experiencing and what he's experi-

[5] Beardsley Ruml, "Some Notes on Nostalgia," *Saturday Review of Literature*, June 22, 1946.

encing, a phase or kind of period we're all going through in our lives. And then my friend said something interesting, that he thought it had to do with the fact that we were all born around 1947 and 1948, that we're all about 25 and should be getting it together in some way. But lots of these people are going through a lot of turmoil right now which makes them very nostalgic for the past due to the transitional stage we're going through and the age we're at.

To interpolate on Ruml's rather vague statement of the thesis, the nostalgic reaction in such situations consists of a psychological inversion of the figure–ground configuration of daily life. Much as in the familiar gestalt silhouette of the vase that suddenly is seen as two faces in profile, the nostalgic reaction similarly inverts that which is figure and that which is ground in our lives. During the developmental transition from adolescence to adulthood it is, on the mundane plane of daily life, the anxieties, uncertainties, and feelings of strangeness about the present and future that constitute *figure* for the youth while *ground* is composed of familiar and likable persons, places, and identities from the past. "Without really changing a thing" (and thus sparing one's being self-accusations of distortion or falsification), the nostalgic reaction inverts the perspective: the warmly textured past of memory that was merely backdrop suddenly emerges as *figure* while the harshly etched silhouette of current concerns fades into *ground.*

The significance of an existentially sharp figure–ground contrast for inducing nostalgic reactions, particularly during late adolescence, is nicely alluded to in Zwingmann's account of the reactions of German and American youth to entering military service during World War II. Noting a much higher rate of acute nostalgic reactions for the American recruits, he goes on to suggest:

[This] was due, in part, to sub-cultural contrast differences between the two nations.

The German boy passes from a male-dominated authoritarian family climate into a male-dominated authoritarian military climate. The contrast is primarily a quantitative one. Furthermore, to serve in the armed forces is a matter of considerable prestige. . . .

The American boy, on the contrary, faces qualitative as well as quantitative changes of traumatic significance. From a democratic main culture and a female-dominated family climate, he passes into a male-dominated authoritarian atmosphere, which has so little prestige that it is used, occasionally, as a prison substitute.[6]

But while the gestalt inversion of an adorned past (from ground to figure) and of an anxious present (from figure to ground) may constitute, as Ruml maintains, the psychological essence of *all* nostalgia it seems that for Western man the transition from adolescence serves, at the mythic level at least, as the prototypical frame for nostalgia for the remainder of life. It is almost as if the depth and drama of the transition were such as to institutionalize adolescence in the personality as a more or less permanent and infinitely recoverable subject for nostalgic exercise. In other words, however "functional" nostalgic indulgence may be for smoothing over the *specific* transition from adolescent to adult, its nostalgic uses do not cease with the completion of this phase of the life cycle. Thus, the fifty-year-old confronting life situations that seem more than normally problematic is as likely to reminisce nostalgically on scenes from adolescence as on ones closer in time, which are perhaps as satisfying and certainly much fresher in memory.

It is not only to the musings of a faceless fifty-year-old that we need turn for evidence of the centrality of adolescent experience for nostalgia's lifelong career, as it were. Myriad novels, poems, plays, and songs at every level of cultural taste (from Goethe to Guest, Schubert to Country-Western, Andy Hardy to Fellini's *Amarcord*) pay homage to adolescence, if not always to the "warm, carefree, fun-filled, first love" imagery of popular sentiment than at least to the labile, bittersweet exudations celebrated in nineteenth-century romanticism. Indeed, some literary and social critics

[6] Zwingmann, "'Heimweh' or 'Nostalgic Reaction'," pp. 215-216.

have held that at the symbolic level there is for Americans no life after adolescence.[7] These critics point out that many of the best American novelists, poets, and playwrights have been wont to picture what follows adolescence as damaged irretrievably by compromise, hypocrisy, corruption, and neglect, that is, spiritual death.

Regardless of whether so grim an ending to the gloss of youth is actually experienced by many Americans, our perduring aesthetic enchantment with adolescence testifies further to the special place it hods for *all* later nostalgic experience and not just for the nostalgia of early adulthood. Thus, for example, the tides of nostalgia which nowadays almost regularly wash over middle-aged persons typically carry them back to the songs, films, styles, and fads of their late teens rather than to those of their childhood or early adult years. In this connection, a rule of thumb for nostalgia merchandisers desirous of intuiting which past period is about to become the subject of the next nostalgia boom would be to subtract twenty years, more or less, from the age cohort about to enter that phase of the life cycle conventionally regarded as constituting full social maturity, that is, persons in their late thirties and early forties. What was new, different, and fashionable—or, better still, slightly outrageous and unconventional—during this cohort's adolescence (typically they are the fathers and mothers of adolescents themselvs) will "all other things being equal"[8] emerge as the symbolic objects of the next mass nostalgia wave.

[7] Most notably Leslie Fiedler, *An End to Innocence* (Boston: Beacon Press, 1955), and in a somewhat different vein Edgar Z. Friedenberg, who in *The Vanishing Adolescent* (New York: Dell, 1962) accuses contemporary American institutions of systematically depriving young people of the joys, escapades, and salutary bewilderments classically associated with that period of life. This makes them, Friedenberg maintains, into hollow men and women well before their time.

[8] The placing of the phrase in quotes is slightly ironic in that, of course, all other things are almost never equal. The phrase obscures such matters as, for example, whether the adolescence of the cohort was historically well marked by some distinguishing, collectively

But, interestingly, what returns as nostalgia for the parental generation constitutes a kind of new experience for the young generation, notwithstanding the latter's probable awareness that what it is witnessing has been around "at least once before." And, as we shall consider in greater detail later, some fascinating possibilities inhere in this situation for the geometry of integenerational time. To a degree, and provided no stronger than usual youth-alienating forces are operative in the culture, it can foster strong symbolic bonds between generations. For example, today's older generation's nostalgic revival of the big-band styles of the early nineteen-forties can, in its own way and for its own ends, capture the imagination of contemporary adolescents so as to produce in them a sympathetic understanding for "what it was like" then, an understanding that would be difficult to impart by words alone.

More intriguing yet, when today's adolescents reach middle age it is probable that their nostalgic revivals will include

---

shared experience, e.g., a depression, a war, an unusual amount of civil disorder? Or was the period marked by some extraordinary turn in popular tastes and life styles, e.g., the abandonment of progressive jazz by the youth of the late fifties and early sixties for rock'n'roll, the noisy arrival on the late sixties scene of the hippie movement with its long hair, flamboyant costuming, recreational drug use, and freer sexual mores? As suggested earlier, strongly figured phenomena of this kind lend themselves more easily to subsequent nostalgic evocation than do less disruptive turns of history. Still another factor to consider is whether the present period is "ripe" for mass nostalgic indulgence. Paradoxically, it appears that, while a strongly figured past makes it a fit subject for present nostalgia, a strongly figured present tends to dissipate the nostalgic resources of the past. War, severe economic hardship, and cataclysmic natural disasters, for example, can so rivet the attention of a people on the present as to stifle "for the duration" any collective nostalgic drift. Much as they are now the objects of popular nostalgic rhapsodizing, the World War II period and the depression of the thirties were not at the time noted for their nostalgic excess. Whether this inhibition at the collective level also interferes with the individual's resort to his own private repository of nostalgic experience is, however, a moot question. Much would depend on how "caught up" he is in the "great events" of his times.

symbolic fragments and residues of what had been the nostalgia of their parents. This second time around, passed-on reflection of their parents' youth is, to be sure, bound to be a highly attenuated version of the original, having upon receipt already been smoothed and prettified through the filter of the parent's nostalgic memory. Similarly, it is likely that even as this once filtered version is assimilated by the new adolescent generation it is being further "adulterated" by images and sensibilities more or less distinctive to the time of its transmittal, e.g., President Kennedy's assassination, the first moon landings, the peculiar spatio-temporal perception of the world afforded by the boxed-in instantaneousness of TV reproduction. But questions of the historical accuracy or contextual fidelity of nostalgia-borne echoes from one generation to the next are, as far as people's collective identity is concerned, a good deal less important than the fact that they occur at all. Indeed, given the severe historical dislocations of the modern world and the rapidity of social change, it seems unlikely that this leapfrogging of nostalgic memory over decades can continue in unbroken fashion for more than a few generations.[9] Modern man, therefore, is perhaps fated to be unrecognizable to his distant progeny in ways that his predecessors were not to theirs.

With respect to the life span of the single individual, however, the symbolic prominence of the adolescent years for

[9] Nonetheless, I would venture that it is through some such inter-generational leapfrogging that it is possible to encounter young people today who, for example, feel a "genuine nostalgia"—as if they had actually lived then—for the tinny jazz sounds, hip flasks, blobbed hair, and flapper dresses of the nineteen-twenties. See the discussion in Chapter 1, "The Nostalgic Experience," on whether it is possible to feel nostalgia for times and places that were not actually part of one's life. For the rather baffling case of Laurence G. Broadmoore, a twenty-four-year-old who is reverentially loyal to the celluloid wing collars, hightop shoes, rolltop desks, wooden swivel chairs, piano rolls, and other paraphernalia of turn-of-the-century America, see Lisa Hammel, "For Young Upstater, the Way It Used to Be Is The Way It Is Again," New York Times, April 3, 1975, p. 32.

later nostalgic experience persists despite the recoil many feel from their own adolescence. As was true of a number of my informants, the adolescent years are often looked on as a time of great emotional pain, confusion, loneliness, insecurity, and awkwardness, giving rise on occasion to such extreme states as recurring doubts concerning one's sanity. But even those of my informants who "confessed" to these feelings nonetheless thought of themselves as somehow wanting and stated their belief that the teens are for most persons a time of fun, romance, adventure, and the exhiliration of self-discovery. Actually, a careful survey might reveal that most adults feel a good deal less enthusiastic about their adolescence than popular stereotypes would suggest. This is yet another example of that species of pluralistic ignorance wherein persons regard themselves as a good deal more atypical than in fact they are. But even if such "data" were made known to the "misled majority," it is unlikely to make much difference in the symbolic importance bestowed on adolescence by Americans. At the level of culture—that is, a people's orienting beliefs and imagery concerning the nature of human experience—adolescence would probably retain its centrality as the main repository for nostalgic materials. Again, by way of explanation, we can only point to the critical and dramatic life changes encompassed by the transition to adulthood and all that this implies for one's subsequent identity.

Such need not be true for all time, however. As cultural anthropologists and culturally oriented psychiatrists never tire of pointing out, there is nothing given in nature or in man that dictates that adolescence must assume the psychosocial prominence it has in Western society or in American society in particular. If it is indeed the case, as Friendenberg maintains, that adolescence is "varnishing"—although possibly for reasons other than those cited by him[10]—then the

[10] Friedenberg, *Vanishing Adolescent*, places the blame mainly on the regimenting tendencies emanting from the sociotechnological

time may not be far off when the nostalgic impulse, the need
to savor a past more yielding to our desires than the present,
will be released from its adolescent moorings to wander more
freely and fancifully over a greater arc of the life span.

Nostalgia in Late Adulthood and Old Age

If nostalgia most savors the adolescnet years, then those
most given to savoring thereof are the aging and the aged—or
so popular thought, not necessarily mistaken, would have it.
"Things aren't what they used to be." "They hardly make
them that way any more." "People no longer take time with
each other." "Nowadays everyone is out for the buck;
nobody cares for the other person any more." "You can
hardly sing the songs they write nowadays, they're all noise
and grunting." And so forth—these are all expressions we
associate with the elderly or those soon to become so.
Indeed, their very utterance is taken as a fairly sure sign of
psychological aging. Moreover, it is not merely the harking
back to the halcyon days of youth that seems so peculiarly
the province of the aged, it is the manner in which this is
done—the wistfulness, the slightly bemused disenchantment
with the current scene, and, most telling of all, perhaps,
the apparent *unquestioned* conviction that the past was
better, that one's belief to that effect is a true reflection of
real change in the world and not some trick of the imagina-

---

sphere of advanced industrial society, particularly from its need for
a skilled, compliant, and mobile labor force. As good a case, however, could be made for the continuing erosion of the traditional
family, the extension of teen-age economic dependence well into
the twenties, greater equality between the sexes along with more
relaxed sexual attitudes, higher levels of social welfare, the muting
of the sharp class distinctions of early industrialism, and an overall
broad advance in the levels of material abundance. All of these
could act as well to profoundly alter the proverbial, romantically
inspired character of adolescence so as to bring about conceivably
its cultural withering away.

tion or the product of a skewed circumstantial perspective. This is patently, or so our view of the aged's nostalgia would have it, pure and simple first-order nostalgia unfettered by any reflexive or interpretative tendency. And, for sure, one does on occasion come upon an old person who almost too perfectly evidences the form, as witness the following lines of the eighty-three-year-old poet and novelist Robert Nathan:

The World That Now
The world that now, in my old age
I go about in,
Is not the world I was born into
Or in which I grew up. It is a world
Changed like the sea in another light,
A storm light. A world
Of raging waves and sudden terror,
Anger . . . and fright.
Legends are lost here, lost and forgotten.
There is no magic here, no ardor—
The full heart, the spirit uplifted—
Its songs are harsh, the sound is deafening.
The young die quickly, without love,
Thrown to the sharks.
We were few, but there were lions among us,
And singing birds.
This is a new world, without beauty,
Without music, without rules.
And everyone is writing,
Telling it like it is, making remarks,
And their books are read by millions
In the drug stores, in the libraries, the schools.
But there is no pride of lions in this world,
No exaltation of larks.[11]

Whether the aging and the aged are in fact as unabashedly or universally nostalgic as popular imagination sees them is of course difficult to say. (I know of no national surveys that have sought to shed light on the question.) But that we so uniformly think of them in this way attests in some pro-

[11] *Los Angeles Times*, Opinion Section, November 13, 1977, p. 7,

found way to our tacit knowledge of what in our society would make them so, as well as perhaps to our *need* to regard them as such.

To consider the latter aspect first, when we write into those life scenarios that we are constantly imagining in our heads the figure of a nostalgic old person prattling on about the beauties and superiorities of decades past, our stance toward him is typically condescending or patronizing. "The poor old duffer is past his prime and of little use to anyone any more. He has nothing to look forward to. What's left him but to dwell on exaggerated memories of 'how beautiful things used to be'?" In fabricating this image, we of course manage simultaneously to assure ourselves of our own vitality, our importance to those around us, our connectedness to the larger world and still bright prospects for the future. Almost irrespective then of whether our picture of the nostalgia-besotted old person is a faithful rendition of what exists, the ego-enhancing uses to which it lends itself in our own lives should be quite apparent.

To turn to the prior question of where such images of the old came from, it is at once obvious that a good deal more than fanciful, self-serving motives account for their propagation. As is unfortunately too often the case with the "folk stereotypes" that social scientists seem forever ready to discredit, there is probably a fair measure of truth in the folk picture of the nostalgic old person. That is to say, there is much about the social regulation of aging and the social condition of the aged in our society that plausibly could account for whatever excessive nostalgia they may indulge in. The array of interrelated casual factors is by now staple in almost any standard sociological text on the aged: the multiple role losses sustained as a result of unemployability due to age discrimination, retirement, income loss, departure of children from home, the death of a mate and of close friends; and all of this along with the progressive attenuation of extended family ties; the rapidity of social change that makes obsolescent such skills, knowledge, and even wisdom as the elderly possess, thus further discrediting them in the eyes of younger persons; the failure of our society, and of modern industrial society generally, to develop genuinely useful and valued social roles for the aged to compensate them for those adult roles it routinely deprives them of; the apparent lack of interest of the aged themselves in organizing politically and in fostering positive collective identities that conceivably could alter their situation of social powerlessness.

Above and beyond the declining health, infirmities and sensory losses inherently associated with growing old, all of the above conspire massively to swamp the last decades with what surely must be a most problematic life transition. Given our theory of the importance of strong existential figure-ground contrasts for evoking nostalgic reactions, small wonder then that the old might be fully as nostalgic as we imagine tham to be. But unlike the nostalgia of the young, that of the old is a nostalgia without end; for, with only an occasional exception, society sees to it that there is no place for them to go but down. Hence the already noted reluctance of the elderly to question the accuracy of their nostalgic memories. Why question that than which life can provide nothing better? And even were it not for the specific social arrangements of our society, which exaggerate the old's inclination toward nostalgic reverie, there is much about the mortal situation *per se*—the knowledge and fear of death's inevitablity—that would in itself so incline them.

Granted, then, that roughly the last third of the normal life span of seventy-some years is a time especially vulnerable to nostalgic affect, there remains the question of what purposes could this possibly serve. The question can be answered on several levels.

Social-structurally, the immersion of the old in nostalgia has the effect of further separating them (in mind in addition to what has already been accomplished in body) from succeeding age grades, who have, or are about to, become role dominant in the society. A structural-functionalist would argue that, all told, this is not such a bad thing in that our "social system" requires little of social value from the aged as a group. Hence, the sooner the psychological analogues of their structural separation from the larger society become operative via nostalgia and other cognitive "adjustments," the better.[12] In any case, it would appear that the nostalgic reverie of the old serves to insulate them to some degree from the severe feelings of rejection and uselessness they would otherwise experience by virtue of their precarious position in the social structure.

Less grimly, it can also be argued that the nostalgia of the elderly acts, politically and historically, to conserve and restore much of value in the culture. The constitutional resistance to statutory and other instrusions on privacy, the preservation of "functionless" historic buildings in the city and countryside, the reintroduction of the soda chair and stained glass windows—to cite a bare few examples, both weighty and trivial—are phenomena of recent years that have been heavily permeated with the nostalgic sentiments of older persons. Of course, radical critics are prone to argue that on balance there is a good deal more of the reactionary than the restitutive in the political uses to which this sort of nostalgia lends itself.

Be that as it may, these are some of the more obvious collective or, in the language of structural functionalism, system relevant uses of nostalgia among the old. This level of analysis shall be explored more fully in a later chapter.

[12] The most extreme form of the argument with respect to the aged is the "disengagement theory" first posited by Elaine Cumming and William H. Henry in *Growing Old: The Process of Disengagement* (New York: Basic Books, 1961). The theory has been much criticized in recent years in large part precisely because of its highly reified functionalist bias. A somewhat softer and more oblique version of the thesis is contained in the very insightful piece by Robert Blauner, "Death and the Social Structure," *Psychiatry* 29 (1966): 378-394.

For now though, what can we say about the subjective uses of nostalgia in the lives of the old themselves, irrespective of how it relates to the political order or the social system?

By and large, there is no reason to believe that nostalgia functions otherwise in their lives than in the lives of younger persons or, for that matter, in the lives of any category of persons, be they age-graded or not. Again, the chief aim is to assuage the uncertainties and identity threats engendered by problematic life transitions. And there is no particular reason to believe that the aged are any less successful in this than are others whose life situations are similarly confounded. What does seem different, however, is that in the case of the elderly their nostalgia, rather than being a transient or episodic response to a problematic life situation, tends to be assimilated into a larger and more continuous process of reminiscence and assessment, termed by some gerontologists the Life Review. According to the psychiatrist Robert N. Butler, this is

> . . . a naturally occurring universal mental process characterized by the progressive return to consciousness of past experiences and, particularly, the resurgence of unresolved conflicts; simultaneously, and normally, these experiences and conflicts can be surveyed and reintegrated. Presumably the process is prompted by the realization of approaching dissolution and death, and the inability to maintain one's sense of personal invulnerability. It is further shaped by contemporaneous experiences and its nature and outcome are affected by the life-long unfolding of character.[13]

Butler goes on to state that whereas for most of the aged the Life Review has positive outcomes—it helps them come to terms with their pasts and to make peace with the present— for some the consequences are distinctly pathological, e.g., severe depression or a marked obsessiveness concerning the remaining months and years of life. The arrogant, those who have injured others, and persons whose adult years were

---

[13] Robert N. Butler, "The Life Review: An Interpretation of Reminiscence in the Aged," *Psychiatry* 26 (February 1963): 66.

marked by a strongly consuming future time orientation are, according to Butler, especially vulnerably to a negative Life Review experience.

Without necessarily subscribing *in toto* to Butler's characterization of the Life Review, in particular to its ostensible universality and its too glib differentiation of "normal" and "pathological" outcomes—actually too little is known about the memory experiences of the elderly to warrant such conclusions—it nonetheless seems reasonable to assume that the process is at least fairly widespread among the aged. And, if this be true, it would seem almost fated for the Life Review to contain a fairly strong infusion of nostalgic sentiment. (Remarkably, Butler barely mentions nostalgia in his article.) This would suggest that the Life Review of the elderly is no simple process of biographical recovery and dispassionate self-assessment, for better or worse, as it were. (The question of the Life Review's historical fidelity, unfortunately, is also not considered by Butler.) On the contrary, even a partially nostalgic rendition of the Life Review opens up possibilities for the embellishment of biographical detail and the muting of latent identity dissonances from one's past. This makes of the process more than mere review; it partakes of a creative act as well.

Yet, as with nearly all occurrences that betoken some special opportunity for creativity, there are in the Life Review attendant dangers as well. These arise mainly from the crass existential circumstance that for the old the life cycle is indeed nearing its end. "There *is* no place left to go," particularly in a secular society such as ours in which few still believe genuinely in an afterlife. And as if this spiritual inability to envision a personal future were not enough, modern institutional arrangements also conspire to thwart even so modest an expectation as the one that a certain wisdom will be transmitted to succeeding generations. Families are smaller; they move about and split apart more frequently; their extended ties are severely attenuated, and the laws and practices of inheritance make it a good deal more difficult to bind successors to one's intentions than was once the case.

Thus, ironically perhaps, those most tempted to submit to nostalgia's balm—the old—are finally those who, in this society at least, probably experience the least relief from its application. The nagging sense of the absence of a future undercuts what is perhaps the chief unspoken aim of nostalgia's exercise, that is, to assuage apprehension of the future by retrieving the worth of the past. This perhaps explains why with the old nostalgia tends so often to drift into bitterness and disillusionment as, for example, in the lines by Robert Nathan cited above. The "algia" part of the condition that Johannes Hofer "diagnosed" three centuries ago, which has all but disappeared in the long etymological interim, reasserts itself here in a new and most poignant way.

*"I offer Rimini in a theatrical sense, scenic and there-
fore inoffensive. . . . My country, as though cleansed,
emptied of its visceral humor, without any aggres-
sivity, without any surprises, reconstructed in the
land of my memory and into which one can enter
without, let us say, the risk of becoming bogged
down."*

> Federico Fellini discussing his film
> Amarcord, *as reported by Nor-*
> *man K. Dorn,* San Francisco
> Sunday Examiner and Chronicle,
> *November 10, 1974*

*Nostalgia for an America that insofar as it ever existed
has now vanished is usually given as the explanation
of the appeal of [Andrew] Wyeth's rural landscapes,
where he shows us an evocative fragment of countryside with a barn or a house, perhaps an animal,
or his even more evocative corners of interiors,
sometimes of a shed with a pail, a basket, or some
other simple object symbolizing American simplicity, thrift and honesty—all this freed (a rather dis-
turbing idea, once it has occurred) from such
impurities as the sound of the hired hand's transistor
radio in the cowshed or Wyeth's own sporty automobile parked just outside the area of vision.*

> John Canaday, *"Wyeth: His Nos-*
> *talgia for a Vanished America*
> *is Still a Best Seller,"* New York
> Times, *July 26, 1970*

*Marcel gives as the reason for his intense nostalgic grat-
ification the following explanation: when he actually
lived through important moments of his life, their
reality was sullied by feelings of fatigue, sadness, anxiety or lack of sufficient perspective to estimate their
true meaning. Art, his own recreation of life, con-
denses past and present. He can live outside of time
now, in retrospect, and thus enjoy the true essence
of life.*

> Milton L. Miller, Nostalgia: A
> Psychoanalytic Study of Marcel
> Proust (*Boston: Houghton Mif-*
> *flin, 1956), p. 106*

NOSTALGIA AND ART

THAT ART THRIVES ON NOSTALGIA and that, simultaneously, it does much to shape the form and provide the substance of our nostalgic experience is, perhaps, as evident as it is difficult to explain. But that all of the arts, even one so nondiscursive and nonrepresentational as music, are forever rummaging through the apparently lost beauties of the past would seem incontestable. We need only reflect on the character of our aesthetic experience, on how often the poem, the story, the song, the picture "reminds us of" or "captures exactly" the way we felt then or "makes us feel sad for some lovely time and place we shall never see again." So frequently and uniformly does nostalgic sentiment seem to infuse our aesthetic experience that we can rightly begin to suspect that nostalgia is not only a feeling or mood that is somehow magically evoked by the art object but also a distinctive aesthetic modality in its own right, a kind of code or patterning of symbolic elements, which by some obscure mimetic isomorphism comes, much as in language itself, to serve as a substitute for the feeling or mood it aims to arouse. That is, the composer "knows" what kind of a melody will produce a feeling of nostalgia in his listeners; a painter "knows" what arrangement of objects, quality of light, and manner of visual perspective he must paint on his canvas for this feeling to be elicited in his viewers. In other words, in its culturally crystalized, symbolically transmuted form nostalgia is as much a device of art as an effect of its exercise.

It will be the aim of this chapter then to inquire into the character of this artful device, its sources in experience and the kind of experience it shapes in its own right. We undertake the task, however, gropingly and, in truth, hesitantly; for, despite the seminal insights of such towering figures as John Dewey and Susanne Langer[1] there is still much that eludes and confounds us about the intercourse of art and experience. Touching again on some of the themes developed in Chapter 1, I shall begin by considering how primary nostalgic experience is, at a level once or twice removed, transformed into an aesthetic modality.

Nostalgia as a Form of Consciousness

In Chapter 1 I tried to sketch some of nostalgia's key attributes and how in terms of its emotional coloration it differs from other forms of subjective experience that also draw heavily on memory, for example, recollection, reminiscence, and recall. Another way to approach the problem, and one which in the present context can better comprehend the interplay of nostalgia and art, would be to treat nostalgia as a distinctive *form of consciousness,* a special optic on the world, as it were, different from those we customarily employ in everyday life. If the idea of nostalgia as a form of consciousness can be accepted, then the process whereby nos-

[1] See especially John Dewey *Art as Experience* (New York: Capricorn Books, 1958), and Susanne K. Langer, *Problems of Art* (New York: Scribner's, 1957).

talgic feeling takes the form of an aesthetic modality (only to rediscover itself later as feeling, albeit of a somewhat different temper) can perhaps be better gleaned if not, to be sure, entirely explicated.

But first we must delve further into what it means to speak of nostalgia as a distinctive *form of consciousness*. For guidance I turn again to the immensely suggestive, ground-breaking essay of Alfred Schutz, "On Multiple Realities."[2] Schutz posits the coexistence of a number of different experiential "realities," although not, as some careless readers have assumed, in the Mannheimian sense of differently situated actors in the social structure interpreting the "same" reality differently.[3] Rather, what Schutz means by *multiple* realities are different realms of subjective experience that can be analytically distinguished from each other in terms of their distinctive time perspectives, apprehensions of self, cognitive assumptions, social contexts, and so forth. Actually Schutz designates six dimensions by which to differentiate the "realities," although it is unclear how exclusive or exhaustive he means these categories to be. These are for the actor: tension of consciousness, epoché (fundamental suppositional stance toward the world), form of spontaneity, form of self-experience, form of sociality, and time perspective.

Whatever analytical categories we use, the point is that each "reality" packages our subjective experience of its phenomenological contents differently so that when perchance we move from one to the other, as for example from a dream state to wide-awakeness, we experience something of a shock, a kind of perceptual startle, which tells us we

[2] Alfred Schutz, "On Multiple Realities," in *Collected Papers, Volume I: The Problem of Social Reality* (The Hague: Martinus Nijhoff, 1962), pp. 207–259.

[3] Karl Mannheim, *Ideology and Utopia* (New York: Harcourt, Brace, 1946).

have shifted from—to employ a parallel term of Schutz's—
one "finite province of meaning" to another. By way of
illustration, Schutz discusses and differentiates the experiential realities of science, dreams, and fantasy. In addition he
implies, but does not bother to chart, the existence of such
other distinctively toned realms of experience (i.e., "realities") as religion, law, pornography, theater, games, and the
like. But phenomenologically superior to, and destined
ineluctably to displace, each of these "finite provinces"
is, says Schutz, the *paramount reality of everyday life,*
that primary state of wide-awakeness, with-itness, and casual
practicality with which we carry out our mundane tasks and
under whose jurisdiction all of the other special, more circumscribed "realities" must ultimately be brought. (What
makes the everyday reality *paramount* need not detain us
here, although the explanation is important for an understanding of Schutz's phenomenology.)

By way of illustrating Schutz's approach, and so that my
own application of it to the nostalgic experience will be
better understood, let us consider the first of his six categories, "tension of consciousness," and see what distinctions
he draws when applying it to the "realities" he actually discusses in the essay: those of everyday life, fantasy, dreams,
and science. Whereas the characteristic "tension of consciousness" of *everyday life* is for Schutz the "wide-awakeness"
with which the actor directs his attention to practical tasks
of the moment, for the *dream* reality it is "passive attention," a turning away from life, which, though it involves
perception, is devoid of apperception (consciousness of the
self perceiving). *Fantasy* reality (the apparent contradiction
in terms notwithstanding) has as its characteristic "tension of
consciousness" pure and arbitrary imaginings of an anticipa-
tory sort, in the manner for example of Don Quixote tilting
at windmills. And, whereas the reality of *scientific theory*
also involves a certain turning away from wide-awakeness,
it is of a very different sort from that evidenced in dreams

and fantasy. Here Schutz speaks of immersion in the "theoretic stance," a profoundly questioning attitude in which rules of logic, evidence, and proof reign supreme to the relative exclusion of arbitrary imagination or, for that matter, practical expediency.

Schutz posits similar variations in his considerations of the other five dimensions he cites. Thus, the characteristic "form of sociality" in the world of everyday life is that of the "we-relation," that is, persons working together at common tasks and in joint pursuits; that for *scientific theorizing,* however, is "solitary," in the sense that however much the *doing* of science may involve others, the scientific attitude *per se* is one of detachment from the world, the better to grasp it in its full objectivity. Similarly, whereas the "time perspective" of everyday life is the "vivid present" (that which is before us *now*), in the world of *dreams* the dreamer lacks a position in objective time. The dream content so intermingles past, present, and sometimes future as well that any notion of standard chronological time is hopelessly dissolved.

Much as we may wish to argue over the accuracy and validity of what Schutz subsumes under each of his reality-delineating categories, we can in the end only stand in awe at his intellectual achievement; to wit, the recognition that each of these different realms of subjective experience constitutes a "reality" in its own right, that each possesses its own structural integrity so that ultimately none can be substituted for or reduced to another. And even if in time all realities must give way to the "paramount reality of everyday life," this is not because of some inherent superiority of design in "everyday life." Rather, the other realities must be only temporarily put aside while we, with our fellows, get on with the practical tasks of life. Most of all, the very notion of *multiple* realities can perhaps check that vulgar habit of mind so intimately associated with the modern technological *Weltanschauung,* which tends to derogate and discount all experience that cannot be accounted for in naturalistic terms or in accordance with the canons of positivistic science.[4]

Schutz speaks of realities. For present purposes I have chosen the alternative term *form of consciousness,* in part because it better conveys the notion of a more or less distinctive organization of inner experience and in part because it avoids the ambiguity of Schutz's use of the term "reality." The ambiguity arises from two sources: (1) the fact that in the main he intends to circumscribe the word's referent to the sphere of inner experience, a usage which unfortunately jars with everyday English in which the referent for reality tends, perhaps with a certain philosophical naiveté, to be located well outside the actor's subjectivity, and (2) Schutz's own habit of occasionally breaking from the peculiarly circumscribed referent he assigns to the term and extending it into realms characterized by organizational structures and social processes, which simply cannot be contained within the sphere of the actor's subjectivity. Thus at points he speaks of the *world* of art, the *world* of religious experience, the play *world* of the child, and so forth.[5] Not only do these "worlds" strike one as being of somewhat different orders, but short of mistakenly attributing to Schutz (by virtue of his generally idealist position) some extreme solipsistic stance, to conceive of them as "worlds" at all would call for many more concepts and categories than the six used by Schutz to differentiate his "realities."

This definitional digression aside, it is clear that in his

---

[4] An even more radical version of the idea of multiple realities, one containing many more evaluative and prescriptive components than Schutz probably would have condoned, is to be found in the quasi-allegorical writings of Carlos Castaneda, *The Teachings of Don Juan: A Yaqui Way of Knowledge* (Berkeley: University of California Press, 1968), and *idem, Journey to Ixtlan* (New York: Simon & Shuster, 1972).

[5] Schutz, "On Multiple Realities," p. 232 *et passim.*

essay Schutz's main concern is to render these "realities" as alternative forms of consciousness or cognitive styles rather than as "worlds" or "organized structures" whose analysis would inevitably necessitate categories exterior to the actor's consciousness as well. Having by this perhaps circuitous route taken some exception to Schutz while still registering our profound indebtedness to him, we can at last pose that question so awkwardly held in abeyance until now: if in its artistic manifestations nostalgia can be conceived of as a form of consciousness, what are its main features?

Recognizing that points of uncertainty and ambiguity will inevitably arise during the course of the exercise, let us nonetheless try to apply Schutz's categories:

1. *Tension of consciousness:* unlike the wide-awakeness of the sphere of everyday life, a *mild detachment* seems to characterize the nostalgic state. The outside world is there, to be sure, and we are even conscious of its existence; but it does not command our full and lively attention as does the onrushing world of moment-to-moment affairs.

2. *Epoché:* essentially no different from that of everyday life wherein the actor suspends such doubts as he might harbor in fancy or theory concerning the "reality" of things, persons, and places "out there." In the nostalgic mood, however, the suspension of disbelief applies somewhat more focally to things past, that is, a selected past acquires a vividness and meaning which make it seem "more real" than it did at the time of its occurrence.

3. *Form of spontaneity:* if *working* be the form of spontaneity of everyday life (i.e., the launching, pursuit, and completion of tasks and projects, however grand or mundane), in the nostalgic state it is clearly musing or reminiscing.

4. *Form of experiencing one's self:* in the mode appropriate for everyday life it is, Schutz says, the *working self functioning as the total self;* that is, the person is so focused on the task at hand that the self is experienced in terms of minute-to-minute demands and relevancies. By contrast, the

musing self in nostalgia assumes, as we suggested in Chapter 1, an *appraising* or, more pointedly, an *appreciative* stance toward the self; a backward-cast yearning, which flatters what we were and where we were then.

5. *Form of sociality:* this is one of Schutz's more ambiguous categories although by it he seems to be pointing to the mode of social interaction that prototypically orients us to, or conveys to us, the interpersonal essence of the "reality" in question. Thus in the realm of everyday life, even as we may pursue our tasks and projects alone, it is with others in mind that we proceed. The world we share with them within which our projects acquire meaning and our regard for what they might think, say, and feel (what Schutz terms the *we-relation*) serve as constant beams to inform and guide our activity. In nostalgia the we-relation that permeates the social sensibility of everyday life would seem to be liberated somewhat. In imagination we allow ourselves convictions of "how lovely it was then" while at the same time exempting ourselves from any immediate or even short-term necessity of documenting the claim or checking it out with others. But this freedom to reconstruct the past is not of the same boundless dimension as Schutz posits, for example, for the realms of fantasy or dreams. Nostalgic memory is in the end, as was pointed out earlier, constrained by a *lived past;* its materials must be *sufficiently* "true" to our pasts to make our romanticized version of them credible to ourselves, even if only momentarily. Hence, and assuming we have not misconstrued this category of Schutz's, it would be fair to say that the form of sociality permeating nostalgia is, like that of everyday life, a *we-relation,* but one modified slightly by a greater measure of imaginative freedom and indeterminacy.

6. *Time perspective:* here, finally, we come to that which most obviously differentiates nostalgia as a form of consciousness. Unlike the "vivid present" of everyday life—that intersection of clock time and our inner time sense—

nostalgia leaps backward into the past to rediscover and revere it. Here present clock time loses much of its relevance, and because the rediscovered past is clothed in beauty temporal boundaries are extended in imagination well beyond their actual chronological span. (The summer's romance is felt to have lasted a year or more.)

To sum up, nostalgia as a form of consciousness can be characterized in Schutzian terms as: a heightened focus on things past (time perspective) along with an enhanced credence in them (epoché), accompanied by considerable musing (form of spontaneity), mild detachment from the affairs of everyday life (tension of consciousness), an essentially appreciative stance toward the self (form of experiencing the self) and attenuation of that sense of we-ness (form of sociality) which in everyday life frames and constrains our conduct. The formulation is admittedly awkward, as must be any attempt to render denotatively and analytically what is *ab initio* a feeling, a mood, or some elusive mental state.[6]

Aesthetic Modalities and Nostalgic Consciousness

Conceding, then, the inherent difficulty of rendering nostolgic consciousness in didactic prose, it is nonetheless our thesis that aesthetic equivalents of this form of consciousness exist in the artist's communication and elicitation of nostal-

[6] Schutz, much more than most social scientists, is painfully aware of the dilemma inherent in putting forward abstract formulations of everyday actions, attitudes, and situations. He points out that, while the abstraction must, if it is to have any validity at all, draw directly on the substance of everyday life, its formulation *per se* inevitably drains the experience of its vividness and spontaniety. Or, as he states it in a slightly different context, puppets (homunculi) come to serve in place of human beings. See Alfred Schultz, "Common-Sense and Scientific Interpretation of Human Action," in *Collected Papers, Volume I,* especially p. 41.

gic sentiment from audiences. A crucial difference, of course, is that the artist's use of the form, unlike the social scientist's, need not get bogged down in difinitional and analytical considerations. He or she "knows" by training, intuition, and prior exercise what configuration of lines, pigments, sounds, movements, or words will touch nostalgic "chords" in the audience. The audience, too, without necessarily having any immediate or "real" reason for feeling nostalgic, will upon seeing or hearing the material respond nostalgically since it, too, has through long associative exposure assimilated the aesthetic code that evokes the emotion. As Meyer states the matter generally for music: "Thus particular musical devices—melodic figure, harmonic progressions, or rhythmic relationships—become formulas which indicate a culturally codified mood or sentiment."[7]

Drawing then on everyday life and feeding back into it in a manner which can at times significantly affect its very course, the expressive distillate of mundane nostalgic experience is part of the *language* of art. And in thus speaking of the *language* of art we, of course, are aware that, compared to the words and phrases of everyday speech, the referential status of nostalgia's symbols, like most other symbolic forms in the arts, is a good deal more vague and ambiguous. (Indeed, it could be argued that to some important degree this heightened vagueness and ambiguity of reference are precisely what make for art rather than mere communication.)[8]

What then are the aesthetic "equivalents" (or perhaps we should term them "translations") for the more or less dis-

[7] Leonard B. Meyer, *Emotion and Meaning in Music* (Chicago: University of Chicago Press, 1956), p. 267. Incidentally, Meyer's book is a particularly valuable reference for exploring the question of what artistic expression in general (not just in music) "means" and how such meaning is accomplished.

[8] For an illuminating discussion of this question see E. H. Gombrich, "Expression and Communication," in *Meditations on a Hobby Horse* (New York: Phaidon, 1963), pp. 53–69.

tinctive form of consciousness that is nostalgia? Clearly, this is terrain that could much more knowledgeably be staked out by the musicologist, the art historian, and the literary critic. Yet, since I am not aware of their having done so with respect to nostalgic sentiment specifically, perhaps some beginnings can be made through the groping and rather crude probes into the problem that follow.

In modern Western music, for example, if one can infer from such "obviously" nostalgic compositions as, to mention but a scant few, Fauré's *Pavanne,* Rachmaninoff's *Vocalise,* the E Minor Prelude of Chopin, Grieg's *Homesickness,* Samuel Barber's *Knoxville Summer of 1915,* the rondo from Beethoven's *Pastoral Sonata* for piano, and portions of the *Enigma Variations* of Elgar, it would seem that the nostalgic modality involves such conventions as a long legato line in a minor key along with such other elements as slow tempi, much rubato, considerable repetition of cadence, and a wavering pulsation of melody, which in vocal music reaches toward a lullaby-like swaying.

In twentieth-century representational painting, as the observations of John Canaday on Andrew Wyeth at the opening of the chapter suggest, nostalgic feeling is often communicated through such devices as a highly filtered quality of light, a photograph-like freezing of movement (as in many of the nostalgic-melancholic canvases of Edward Hopper), and ironically—since we often associate nostalgia with vagueness and murkiness—a tendency to outline objects sharply so that they stand out "in memory" perhaps even more clearly than they did in "real life." (This is perhaps the aesthetic analog of what Schutz terms the epoché, which in nostalgia involves, as we said, a qualitative shift in our disposition to make the memory of the past even less subject to cognitive doubt than our awareness of the present.)

Similarly, in Western dance, perhaps more in modern than in classical ballet, certain conventions are employed that seem to "capture" the yearning for a cherished past. One thinks almost instantly of those slow, long-strided, dance steps of sharply bent knee, along with the languorous, undulating arm movements, which one associates for example with the dances of Martha Graham. In theater (a play like Tennessee Williams's *The Glass Menagerie* comes readily to mind) such means as scrim, half-light, echoes, distantly tinkling sounds, silhouetted figures, and body movements of peculiar deliberateness are employed to convey the protagonist's nostalgic recapturing of moments and matters past. In cinema, too, since so many of its techniques still derive from stagecraft, very similar devices, along with appropriate mood music, are invoked to register nostalgia. The nostalgic effect is further heightened when on occasion the film cleverly plays on the audience's subliminal sense of what old photographs and early cinematography looked like. Thus, the "turning back" to grainy black-and-white, pre-technicolor cinematography in *The Last Picture Show* and, somewhat less credibly, to sepia color in sections of *Butch Cassidy and the Sundance Kid* seem to heighten considerably the nostalgic mood of those films. (But not all so-called nostalgia films follow these particular symbolic conventions, as we shall note shortly.)

And, finally, fiction and poetry contain their own aesthetic conventions for communicating nostalgia. Despite their being much more constrained than, for example, music and painting by the requirements of denotative and didactic communication, these arts nonetheless possess a variety of resources of their own for casting a nostalgic "spell" over the reader. Without pretending to be at all definitive on the matter (after all, rhetoricians and literary critics from Aristotle to Kenneth Burke have tried to analyze which conventions and configurations produce which emotional effects in the reader or listener) but merely by way of adducing the general point, one need only cite such nostalgia-evoking devices as, in poetry, the alliterative, somewhat prolix cadence ("when to the sessions of sweet silent thought

I summon . . . ") or, in fiction, the preference for the first person, the past continuous tense, and intransitive verbs ("For a long time I used to go to bed early.") over the simple past or past perfect tense.

This brief examination of nostalgic means, devices, and approaches in the several arts is, of necessity, more illustrative than definitive, more selective than exhaustive. It cannot in and of itself establish the existence of wholly distinctive and differentiated nostalgic modalities in the arts; neither can it claim to have considered sufficiently the full range and variety of nostalgia-evoking possibilities in any particular art. Rather, what I have tried to do is to advance the plausibility of the thesis that nostalgia, because of its prominence and pervasiveness as a distinctive mind-body state, enters inevitably into the language of all of the arts, both those more discursive[9] and those more expressive. And, in so doing, nostalgic feeling comes to assume certain conventional expressive forms in the arts. What specific form these will take will, of course, depend greatly on culture and history, not least of all on the expressive traditions that have prevailed historically in a particular art *per se*. But the inference that such conventions do exist for nostalgia in some recognizable and communicable from would seem to be warranted, if for no other reason, on the basis of our aesthetic experience alone.

Granted, then, that each art form probably includes in its aesthetic repertoire certain more or less distinctive conventions for communicating nostalgia (just as it includes still other conventions for communicating other common sentiments), two sorts of questions remain, in line with the broader sociological frame of this inquiry, to be considered. The first has to do with how fixed or immutable these

---

[9] The term is taken from Langer's discussion of discursive and non-discursive symbols in the arts and in communication generally. See Susanne K. Langer, *Philosophy in a New Key* (New York: New American Library, 1951), pp. 75–94.

conventions are and whether the range of expressive materials that they may draw upon is restricted in some significant way by certain inherent attributes of the emotion that the artist wishes to evoke. For example, is music "fated" for all time to express the quenched yearning of nostalgia through the modality of a long, wavering, legato melodic line? The second type of question touches on the thorny issue of how nostalgic expression is differentiated, if at all, in "popular" as against "high" culture or, from a slightly different vantage point, in "folk" as against "sophisticated" art.

Stability or Modifiability of Aesthetic Conventions: The Case of Some Recent Hollywood Nostalgia Films

In its general form the question perhaps need hardly be asked. The history of art alone attests to the striking modifications in aesthetic conventions that have been wrought over the centuries and will most certainly continue to be wrought for as long as an institutional complex called "the arts" exists. From Classicism to Romaticism, from Abstract Expressionism to Pop Art, from minimalism to conceptualism, from Gothic to Baroque to Rococo, from diatonic tonality to chromaticism to atonality, and so forth and so on—in addition to whatever else these shorthand labels signify, they point to the recurrent overhauling of established aesthetic perceptions, cognitions, and relations and their replacement by new and different ones, often including the rediscovery of some that had been discarded unceremoniously as "obsolete" in some earlier artistic revolution. Indeed, to the degree that one subscribes to the view that a major function of art is to cause us to experience the mundane and taken-for-granted in new, freshly illuminating ways, then it follows that art must of necessity, particularly as the conditions of life change, ceaselessly modify and transform its expressive modalities. This, of course, is not to deny the existence of profound continuities in art as well, but only to point up that strange yet increasingly common experience of modern life wherein that which "made no sense" to our eyes and ears at first—and may even have constituted something of an affront to them—comes in relatively short order to be regarded as "just right" and even "beautiful." In like measure that which pleased us a short while ago now seems "shallow" or "old-fashioned" or simply "not right somehow"—"whatever could I have seen in that, I wonder"?[10] And of such things, naturally, are the little and big revolutions in art made, not to speak of the making and unmaking of the artistic élites that come to be associated with one style or another.

Even were we to grant then—and it would be rash to do so—that the artistic symbolization of an emotion such as nostalgia is subject ultimately and perennially to some irreducible stylistic constraint by virtue of its affective properties *per se*[11] it would still be exceedingly arbitrary (and patently contrary to historical experience) to claim that the aesthetic molds for shaping nostalgia are, as it were, frozen for all time or, even for a particular cultural epoch. The *feeling* of nostalgia may remain the same for all times, places, and peoples, but the artistic idiom that evokes it in one era may evoke something quite different, or nothing at all, in another. Conversely, genres, styles, and conceits

---

[10] Fashion changes are the clearest and most widespread example of this phenomenon. In this sense, fashion can be thought of, particularly for moderns, as the primordial conversion experience. More than by any other medium, religion and art included, fashion is the means whereby our perception and experience of large segments of our everyday world are constantly being recast.

[11] This would be equivalent to a claim in music, for example, that however else the composer might choose to express nostalgia, he *never* could render it in fortissimo, intensely rhythmic, rapid, staccato-like passages (e.g., the *Sabre Dance* from Khachaturian's *Gayne Ballet Suite*); or, in painting that the nostalgic mood could ever be evoked by rigorously geometric, hard-edged shapes of strong primary color (as in the works of Pieter Mondriaan or Frank Stella).

that in one epoch strike one as leagues removed from nostalgic sentiment can, at a later time, capture it to a turn.[12] But having said this, we should not be led to an easy acceptance of the opposite, equally rash and unsubstantiated inference, namely—and to the regret and ruin of many a fashion designer and other artistic "innovator"—that the genres and idioms for expressing some mood or sentiment are wholly arbitrary and can be altered at will or by "authoritative decree."[13]

In this connection several Hollywood nostalgia films of the early nineteen-seventies are revealing of the hazards and ambiguities attendant to an attempt to switch artistic metaphors. In cinema, perhaps because the camera can do a much better job of bringing us close into the visual field of action than is possible in theater, there has been from early on—at least as far back as von Stroheim's 1924 masterpiece *Greed*— a latent tendency to formulate an alternate convention for nostalgia, one that rejects the essentially impressionistic approach inherited from stagecraft. I refer to that genre which eschews the visually vaporous and existentially distanced and opts instead for a heightened, almost obsessive realism that strains to recapture *exactly*, in minute and exquisite detail, how objects looked then, how people spoke and dressed then, what was uppermost on their minds then, and so forth. Paying fit homage to the truth claims of nostalgic sentiment, filmmakers of this bent seem to ask, "Why

---

[12] The tinny, victrola-squelched jazz band sounds of the twenties, which for a long time signified the tawdry and dissolute (e.g., Kurt Weil's music for the *Dreigroschenoper*) since World War II have come more and more to serve in dramatic scores and musical theater as the signature of nostalgia. An early premonition of this idiomatic transformation occurs in *Private Lives*, where Noel Coward has one of his characteristically wistful heroes remark, "Strange, how potent cheap music is."

[13] I draw here on the somewhat dated but still seminal discussion of fashion by Herbert Blumer in his article "Collective Behavior," in A. M. Lee, ed., *New Outline of the Principles of Sociology* (New York: Barnes & Noble, 1946), pp. 216–218.

can't we recapture the past *exactly as it was* rather than through a glass darkly?"[14] Indeed, the evergrowing swell of the nostalgia wave of the early nineteen-seventies brought with it quite a few films that, superficially at least, strove after this, among them such striking boxoffice successes as *American Graffiti, The Way We Were, They Shoot Horses, Don't They?* and *The Sting.*[15]

In principle there is, as I have argued, no reason why the cinematic convention for nostalgia should not shift from an impressionistic to a hyperrealistic idiom, just as, for example, a similar shift occurred in American painting sometime during the nineteen-thirties from an impressionistically based nostalgia to the "magic realism" of Hopper, Wyeth, and Wood. Yet, in addition to whatever else was right or wrong with the films cited above, they were artistic failures as "*nostalgia* films," despite the fact that this is what they set out to be. How so? Because to establish a new aesthetic convention or idiom for an old sentiment requires something more than a mere recasting of the sentiment into another form. The *act* of recasting itself—whatever the new mold is to be, impressionistic, expressionistic, or naturalistic—must somehow be bracketed or framed[16] so that the audience's sense of viewing the world through a new optic (in this case *the frame* of hyperrealism) is enlivened and made

---

[14] But, of course, the punctilious concern for naturalistic exactitude is itself "unnatural" and is as much a convention as its opposite. In the words of Schutz it, too, represents a perceptual shift from that "paramount reality of everyday life" whose concern for verisimilitude is actually a good deal more casual than fastidious. To submit finally to the aesthetic dictates of a hyperrealistic idiom also entails shifting to a nonordinary form of consciousness or, as Schutz would have it, to "another reality." Schutz, *Collected Papers, Vol. I*, pp. 207–286.

[15] I am indebted to Chandra Mukerji for pointing out to me the pervasiveness of nostalgic "hyperrealism" in these and numerous other films of the period.

[16] The importance of "frame" devices for the organization of ongoing experience is thoroughly elucidated in Erving Goffman, *Frame Analysis* (New York: Harper, 1974).

subjectively articulate. Put differently, the essential "as if" perspective underlying all aesthetic experience must remain inviolate no matter what transmutation of style, idiom, or genre is entailed in the abandonment of one artistic convention for another.

It was precisely this failure to place the hyperrealistic genre cinematically in quotation marks, as it were—some device to allow the audience to adopt an "as if" perspective on the historic past it had so recently traversed—that confounded, and finally, adulterated whatever genuine nostalgic emotion the films sought to evoke. *American Graffiti* especially ("Where were you in '62?" the trailers and advertisements, brashly asked), and *The Way We Were* and *They Shoot Horses, Don't They?* to nearly the same degree were, in the vernacular, altogether too "up front." Once their crude period identifications of time and place had been established,[17] the metaphorically impoverished hypernaturalism to which these films gave vent, rather than evoke a nostalgic sense of the past, made events appear as but a slightly oblique version of the present. That a hypernaturalistic convention for nostalgia in film may yet displace the long-established, more impressionistically inclined idiom is of course still possible and perhaps only awaits the arrival of one or two creative filmmakers who can better exploit this aesthetic tendency. Until then, however, films like *The Last Picture Show, Amarcord,* and, in their more nostalgic moments, *Bonnie and Clyde* and *Jules and Jim,* all of which manage to retain a peculiarly contemplative distance from their pasts, are likely to remain preeminent in this genre.

[17] As for *The Sting,* the problem of hypernaturalism's artificiality is further confounded by the cavalier imposition of pre-World War I ragtime music and "big store" con games onto the chic gangsterism of the twenties and the social protest atmosphere of the thirties. In short, the film was a historical mess, despite the apparently obsessive care taken by its makers to have everything look "extra-real."

Nostalgia in Popular and High Culture

These observations on how bracketing engenders new aesthetic conventions lead quite naturally to the second of the two questions posed some pages back, namely, the differences, if any, in nostalgic expression in popular vs. high culture or in folk vs. sophisticated art. The question itself touches, in turn, on the discussion in Chapter 1 of the ascending orders of nostalgic experience—the simple, the reflexive, and the interpretative.

To the considerable degree that it engages nostalgic themes, popular art in Western culture tends by and large to confine itself to simple, first-order nostalgic representations, which unabashedly wax on the beauties of the past and proclaim, rather naively as a rule, their superiority over present conditions. By contrast, so-called high or serious art, while by no means averse to fashioning nostalgic pleas, at the same time usually asks its audience to adopt a more tentative, even ambivalent, stance toward such representations. That is, through a variety of devices (ambiguities, asides, contradictions, veiled suggestions) it invites the audience to question the truth—or, at least, the whole truth—of nostalgic memory and perhaps even to ponder why one might feel nostalgic at all. Significantly, the serious artist seems somehow constrained to pose such reflexive questions even though he or she chooses not to answer them or is at a loss to know how to. Chekhov, for example, is notorious for posing agonizing questions on the relationship of present disenchantment to remembered beauty and fantasized promise. But these are questions for which his plays provide no answer or, at best, only the most enigmatic of answers. A gifted English novelist, the late Elizabeth Bowen, has pointedly expressed the reluctance of the serious artist to avail herself of an easy resort to simple nostalgic sentiment:

> A very great part of the writing of our own period has served as a carrier—yes, and promoter too of this nostalgia. Would such writ-

ing succeed—which is to say, be acceptable—if there were not a call for it? I suppose, no. One of the dangerous powers of the writer is that he feeds, or plays up to, desires he knows to exist. He knows of their existence for the good reason that they are probably active in himself. In contacting the same desires in his readers he does something to break down his isolation. If, by so doing, he also may make his living, who is to blame him? But without injustice to him, we should recognize this: that it is easier to recall than to invent, easier to evoke than to create.

It is true, of course, that creation in the literary sense is, must be, to a great extent evocation, the calling up of images, feelings, trains of thought which are recognizable, being common to all men. Accepted human experience is not only the writer-artist's subject; it gives him his terms of reference, and up to a point provides—even dictates—his vocabulary. But am I wrong in saying the inner object of art is not merely to reproduce, but to add?[18]

Is if off the mark then to suggest that in serious or sophisticated art the "addition" of which Bowen speaks consists not so much in the avoidance of nostalgic sentiment as in the more creative act of placing it in a problematic context, that is, elevating it from a simple first-order expression to a second (reflexive) or third (interpretative) -order expression?

Interestingly, one of the favored means in Western art for accomplishing this, particularly in the less discursive arts of music, dance, and painting, has been to purposefully exploit elements of the popular of folk idiom which in its own context displays the very qualities of simplicity, naiveté, and gross sentimentality that we assoicate with the form. To wit: the "primitivism" of Picasso is not that of the primitive, the Campbell soup cans of Andy Warhol are not those in the magazine ad, and the folk songs in Bartok's music are not those sung by Hungarian peasants. What the artist has done in these instances, and in innumerable others that could as easily be cited, is to *bracket* (to place in quotation marks,

[18] Elizabeth Bowen, "The Cult of Nostalgia," *The Listener*, August 9, 1951, p. 224.

as it were) the naive (first order) modality and thereby critically alter its meaning, much as the placement of tongue in cheek alters the meaning of the spoken word. Whether the intent be ironic, denunciatory, or even celebrative (as Rousseau, for example, celebrates the noble savage), the effect is to heighten our awareness of the naive folk or popular idiom and thereby to place us in a new (no longer naive) relationship to it. (Again, the wailing saxophone sounds in the Brecht-Weil *Three Penny Opera,* however close they come musically to nineteen-twenties jazz, are not evocatively the same as those played by real jazz bands of the period; nor, for that matter—and much more obviously—are the "jazz" compositions of Milhaud, Ravel, and Stravinsky the "same" as the popular jazz music of the period.)

In sophisticated art a highly conscious and sometimes playful element of "as-if"-ness is interposed between the naive symbol and its referent by virtue of the bracketing or framing operation. This allows us to view critically that which we formerly either took too much for granted or dismissed too readily and thoughtlessly—much as "highbrow" critics once cavalierly dismissed jazz—as artistically unworthy. The semantic subtleties and convolutions of which this process of bracketing (and successive rebracketing of the brackets) is capable is nicely captured by the fashion writer Kennedy Fraser in her commentary on the spring 1975 Paris fashions:

> What the support for flea-marketry represents more, perhaps, than affection for the secondhand is the desire to find style, but obliquely, and splendor, but tackily, and so put an ironic distance between the wearers and the fashionableness of their clothes. The ironic approach is an essential part of style in clothes by now—an air of saying something quite intense but only in a footnote. This approach has grown up out of flea-market and "nostalgic" fashion.[19]

The bracketing process also carries with it the remarkable

[19] *The New Yorker,* April 14, 1975, pp. 84–85.

secondary consequence that once we have assimilated the
metaphoric transposition the original object can no longer be
quite the same for us; after Warhol, never can we again see
Campbell soup cans on the grocer's shelf in quite the same
way as before, just as after Klee the stick-figure drawings of
children can no longer be seen exactly as before. Eventually,
to be sure, for those who follow us, although sometimes
within the span of our own lives as well, the parenthetical
function performed by the bracketing operation withers
away as it, too, is assimilated into the realm of primary,
taken-for-granted experience and loses the startle-inducing
properties it once possessed. Then, as the history of art and
the etymology of metaphors generally demonstrate, new
bracketing mechanisms will be essayed which will start the
cycle all over again.[20]

Just as, then, the bracketing of the primitive, the parenthe-
sizing of the pastoral, the framing of the sentimental elevates
their aesthetic function to where we can experience the
world in fresh and interesting ways, so does the artful transposition of simple nostalgia into something more reflexive
and interpretative alter fundamentally our previously unexamined, merely evocative relationship to the past. No
longer are we on the plane of simple yearning for bygone
scenes and experiences. Still drawing on the reality of that
yearning, we ascend to a higher level at which we become
engaged in an internal dialogue that probes our memories
and reconstructions for their source, their authenticity, and

[20] From this vantage point, the process of reflexive bracketing and
rebracketing in art is not wholly unlike the process of paradigmatic
shifts described by Kuhn for revolutions in science. Except for the
fact that the "empirical referents" for paradigmatic shifts in art are
more obscure, which tends perhaps to make the succession of styles
in art seem somewhat arbitrary, much the same generic stage
process of breakthrough, to normalcy, to conceptual exhaustion,
to new breakthrough can be observed in art as in science. See
Thomas S. Kuhn, *The Structure of Scientific Revolutions* (Chicago:
University of Chicago Press, 1962).

their utility. Different artists will, of course, conduct this perennial dialogue on the past differently and arrive at different conclusions, as varied, for example, as the grim proclamation of the necessity of illusion in the later plays of Eugene O'Neill to the gentle resignation of the old professor in Ingmar Bergman's *Wild Strawberries*. His reflexive nostalgia leads him finally to recognize the extent to which his worldly success was furthered (perhaps inevitably) at the expense of others' feelings. Whatever the conclusion, no message or moral is fated. Whichever emerges, we can see that as one of art's more enduring resources nostalgia need not merely feed upon or revel in the past; it can become the means for creatively using the past as well.

*Alike with the individual and with the group, the past
is being continually re-made, reconstructed in the
interests of the present, and in both cases certain out-
standing events or details may play a leading part in
setting the course of reaction. Just as the individual
recall takes on a peculiar personal tinge, owing to
the play of temperament and character; so that kind
of recall which is directed and dominated by social
conditions takes a colouring which is characteristic
of the special social organization concerned, owing
to the play of preferred persistent tendencies in the
group.*

F. C. Bartlett, Remembering
(Cambridge, England:
Cambridge University
Press, 1932)

*History serves the community in the same way as the
memory does the individual. A person has to bring
up a certain portion of the past to determine what
his present is, and in the same way the community
wants to bring up the past so it can state the present
situation and bring out what the actual issues themselves are. I think that is what history uniformly is.
It is always prejudiced in one sense, that is, deter-
mined by the problem before the community.*

George Herbert Mead, (Chicago: University of Chi-
cago Press The Philosophy
of the Act, 1938)

NOSTALGIA
AND SOCIETY

WHAT DOES IT MEAN for the collective life of a group, a community, a people, for the way we relate to each other and for our existence as a society, that such an emotion as nostalgia exists, that it assumes the forms it does, and that it exhibits itself so vividly in the particular contexts in which it does—in identity formation, through the discontinuities of the life cycle, and in artistic expression? In short, what are the *consequences* of nostalgic experience for society, for that abstract entity whose patterning of ranks, roles, and positions, whose practices, conventions, and beliefs we are wont to infuse with a life and dynamic of its own, above and beyond the irreducible individuality of the myriad persons who can be said to "constitute it" at any particular moment in time.

This is, to be sure, the fundamental sociological question to be put regarding this or any phenomenon that humans, through their language and culture, invest with meaning and sentiment. *What difference does it make "for the whole"*— however variously that whole may be conceived of by different philosophers and social theorists? (But that the societal whole does somehow "exist," if only as a kind of Kantian noumenon, and that it can somehow be "looked after" and "cared for" is a grounding assumption of modern life that laymen now hold to almost as unquestioningly as do philosophers and social theorists.) Among the few social scientists who have studied nostalgia the question has not been entirely neglected, although since most such work has been done by psychologists there has been an understandable tendency to focus on the personal rather than the societal implications of nostalgia. Nonetheless Beardsley Ruml, for example, writing soon after the close of World War II, argues strongly that nostalgic feeling is deeply intertwined with nationalistic and patriotic sentiment and hence serves a particularly important political function in time of war. Generalizing on this theme, he goes on to suggest:

> The understanding of political behavior cannot be complete [if explained solely] in terms of any calculus of self-seeking motives; nor can the nostalgic elements be dismissed as epiphenomenal, incidental and accidental. The nostalgic sentiments are fundamental, essential and ubiquitous and must be given due consideration in political analysis at either the theoretical or practical level.[1]

Alas, Ruml leaves this formidable task to others.

Some years later the existentially inclined psychologist Zwingmann speculates:

> The reason for the assumption that the [calculating] attitude toward time and time-lapse in Western, and particularly American, culture is etiologically related to nostalgic behavior is based on the rationale that a culture which is strongly oriented along utilitarian and materialistic lines makes loss of, or failure to attain, values supporting this orientation (that is, youth, beauty, productivity and the accumulation of physical property) a threat that requires search for gratification in the past.[2]

---

[1] Beardsley Ruml, "Some Notes on Nostalgia," *Saturday Review of Literature*, June 22, 1946, p. 8.

[2] Charles A. A. Zwingmann, "'Heimweh' or 'Nostalgic Reaction': A Conceptual Analysis and Interpretation of a Medico-Psychological

Zwingmann seems to be suggesting that at the societal level nostalgia functions as a kind of safety valve for disappointment and frustration suffered over the loss of prized values.

Even among writers not concerned with nostalgia as such, one occasionally comes upon a particularly striking account of its role in social and historical change. Thus in a recent book the social historian Raymond Williams seeks to demonstrate that the centuries-long nostalgia for rural life in Britain has served to obscure, in terms of both political action and political theory, the grievous extent to which capitalism was responsible for the miseries and excesses ushered in by nineteenth-century industrialism.[3] In a like vein the sociologist Gerald Suttles points an accusing finger at urban America's nostalgia for the "old ethnic neighborhood" as squelching the possibilities for a creative, democratic reconstitution of the American city:

Nonetheless there is a nostalgia for a past in which interpersonal relations and territorial solidarities were more fixed because they were thought to be outside the realm of human choice. This nostalgia has given rise to a resurgence of primordial groups and at least a loud outcry on the part of new separatists. These developments are paralleled by an intellectual analysis of territorial groups which reasserts the limits of human nature to expand loyalties past local and parochial groups. This nostalgia for the past and for a more permanent sense of community and interpersonal loyalty is expectable where large numbers of people throughout the world are being urged out of their local confines and for the first time included in mass society. Social analysis of this nostalgia and the movement growing out of it, however, need not follow in its steps and reaffirm the unalterable character of small-scale localized collectives.[4]

Phenomenon," unpublished Ph.D. dissertation, School of Education, Stanford University, 1959, p. 227.

[3] Raymond Williams, *The Country and the City* (New York: Oxford University Press, 1974).

[4] Gerald D. Suttles, *The Social Construction of Communities* (Chicago: University of Chicago Press, 1972), pp. 187–88. In an article titled "Ethnicity: The Last Hurrah of Nostalgia," *Los Angeles*

Indeed, the note sounded by Williams and Suttles is a more elegant rendering of what over the years has come to be an almost clichéd denunciation by left-leaning liberals and radicals of nostalgia; namely, that it is at best a fatuous indulgence of the elderly fearful of even mild social change of a progressive cast and, at worst, a kind of moral soporific of the masses that blinds them to the true class enemy and blunts their radical zeal. In these more extreme fulminations it is almost as if the emotion itself were *the* palpable villain, much as we are prone at times to anthropomorphize some "deadly" sin like cupidity or sloth. The radical polemicist utters the word with a sneer as if its perfidiousness were contemptible as well as transparent. But that radical leftists, too, can be deluded by their own brand of nostalgia is vividly suggested by the iconoclast writer Tom Wolfe:

> The New Left had a strictly old-fashioned conception of life on the streets, a romantic and nostalgic one somehow derived from literary images of *proleterian* life from before World Warr II or even World War I. A lot of the white college boys, for example, would go for those checkered lumberjack shirts that are so heavy and wooly that you can wear them like a jacket. It was as if all the little lord byrons had a hopeless nostalgia for the proleteriat of about 1910, the Miners with Dirty Faces era, and never mind the realities—because the realities were that by 1968 the real hardcore street youth in the slums were not into lumberjack shirts, Can't Bust 'Ems and Army surplus socks. They were into the James Brown look. They were into ruffled shirts and black-belted leather pieces and bell-cuff herringbones, all that stuff, mucking around, getting over looking sharp—heading toward the high-heeled Pimpmobile *got to get over* look of . . . 1973. If you tried to put one of those lumpy mildewed mothball lumberjack shirts on them—these aces—they'd vomit.[5]

Times, June 22, 1977, Section II, p. 7, almost identical cautions are sounded by Irving Howe, himself partially responsible for an efflorescence of ethnic Jewish nostalgia as a result of his superb and highly successful book on the East European Jewish immigrant experience in America, *World of Our Fathers* (New York: Harcourt Brace Jovanovich, 1976).

[5] Tom Wolfe in his introduction to René Konig, *À La Mode: On the Social Psychology of Fashion* (New York: Seabury Press, 1973), p. 27.

Regardless of the partisan stance one assumes with respect to the emotion (pro or con, denunciatory or indulgent) there does seem to be some appreciation of the fact in both lay and intellectual circles that nostalgia is deeply implicated in the political life of a people and in their historical sense of themselves. But how is it implicated? Whereas a good empirical answer to this question would require many concrete, close-in historical and psychological studies about matters that writers like Williams, Suttles, and Wolfe take mainly for granted, the sociologist on the basis of his knowledge of how societies are held together can begin to sketch the *broad* outlines of such an answer. Recognizing the tentativeness of such an undertaking, I wish to essay such a crude sketch here.

To begin, I would point to two aspects of nostalgic experience discussed earlier, which I believe are essential for any proper understanding of its relationship to society at large. These are: its sources in the perceived threats of identity discontinuity and its role in engendering *collective* identities among people generally, but most especially among members of "the same generation."[6]

Identity Discontinuity and Collective Experience

Just as the phasing of the life cycle periodically entails status transitions that in their perceived discontinuity and attendant anxiety evoke nostalgic reactions from individuals,

---

[6] I place the phrase in quotes because only slight reflection is called for to realize that inasmuch as the birth, replacement, and death of a population is a continuous process, what makes for "a generation" and what distinguishes it from preceding and subsequent generations are by no means simple questions. Indeed, as we shall soon see, nostalgic experience is a primary vehicle in the generation-defining process. For a more general treatment of the question, however, see the classic essay of Karl Mannheim, "The Problem of Generations," in Mannheim, *Essays on the Sociology of Knowledge* (London: Oxford University Press, 1952).

so do untoward major historic events and abrupt social changes pose a similar threat and evoke a similar response from people in the aggregate. The difference, of course, is that historic events and social changes are not institutionally scheduled into the flow of our lives as are the phased events of the life cycle. Nonetheless, even though a noteworthy historic event or profound social change may seem to lie farther outside the mainstream of our lives than, for example, our adolescence, parenthood, or old age, what it lacks in immediacy is often made up for subjectively by the feelings of surprise and strangeness it induces in us. It is as if we were suddenly made aware of a rent in the larger existential fabric of our being-in-the-world, where formerly we perceived a whole. And this, too, is a form of discontinuity with which we must somehow cope. Moreover, unlike the person's passage through the life cycle, the untoward event, although unanticipated, involves a concentration of attention and anxious concern among millions of persons at the same moment of historical time, thereby creating a fertile social psychological medium for the production and diffusion of nostalgic sentiment. Herein lies, too, as we shall see more fully later, the powerful generation-delineating properties to which nostalgia lends itself so easily: we summon to mind and communicate among ourselves those comforting images from our pasts (e.g., the rumble seat, the lindy hop, the drive-in teen-age hangout, and so forth) which seem to iconically bestow upon that past an age-graded distinctiveness and separableness that mere chronological divisions could never by themselves engender.

But what are the untoward historic events and abrupt social changes of which I speak? Concerning the former I have in mind the familiar litany of wars, depressions, massive natural disasters, deaths and assassinations of great national leaders, which, having jarred our beings, have also marked our epochs. As for the latter, I would merely by way of example cite the *apparent* sudden onset of fuel and food shortages in the early nineteen seventies; the crisis in governmental legitimacy emanating from the Watergate and associated CIA–FBI–IRS scandals of about the same time; the massive eruption of counterculture movements in the late nineteen-sixties; the seemingly abrupt transformation—from roughly the mid-fifties to the mid-sixties—of many an American central city from a thriving, densely peopled business and civic entrepot to a decimated, rubble-strewn urban landscape; the shift in the seventies from an ethos of ever expanding growth and opportunity to a restrictive, conservationist "small is beautiful" outlook.

Still other relatively sudden kinds of social changes from recent and earlier periods could be cited as easily. The important point, however, is that, in contrast to social changes that are more gradual and hence less perceptible in their unfolding, this kind of social change has the capacity of eliciting in us that startle response, that sudden gestalt inversion of existential figure and ground which, as we noted earlier, often occasions the release of nostalgic feeling.[7] It is as if at the moment of recognizing the *new* situation or condition we are led to remark to ourselves and to others, "Hey, isn't this a lot different from what was being seen/said/thought/felt just a few short years ago?"

Allowing then that we are susceptible to feelings of anxiety and concern for our future selves when we are brought up short by some untoward historic event or intrusive social change,[8] it can be seen how at the most elemental level

---

[7] Again, of the few social scientists who have written on nostalgia, Ruml, "Notes on Nostalgia," has been the most illuminating on this facet of the phenomenon.

[8] From one vantage point this is, perhaps, a tautology in that however an historic event or social change is defined "objectively" its definition would ultimately have to admit of some such subjective impact as well. This problem of objective occurrence vs. subjective definition is analagous to that treated by Richard C. Fuller and Richard R. Myers in their famous article "The Natural History of a Social Problem" *American Sociological Review* 6 (June 1941): 320-329.

collective nostalgia acts to restore, at least temporarily, a sense of sociohistoric continuity with respect to that which had verged on being rendered discontinuous. And this period, when the nostalgic reaction waxes strong, may afford just enough time for the change to be assimilated into the institutional machinery of a society (e.g., into the realms of law, politics, religion, and education) as it could not at first and, were it left wholly up to purely *private* feeling, might not for some time thereafter. It may well be, for example, that the apparent ease and rapidity with which such formerly "disgusting and disgraceful" practices as out-of-wedlock cohabitation, nudity, pronography, homosexuality, female assertiveness, and the like, are currently being tolerated and even protected in the *public* sphere is in large part related to the concomitant nostalgia binge which has allowed people to indulge their shaken convictions concerning the superiority and surety of traditional social arrangements and practices.[9] In other words, the former might not be possible without the latter.

The Nostalgia Orgy of the Nineteen-Seventies

This is, probably, a fitting place for inserting a long postponed topic that, while it may not advance a general sociological theory of nostalgia as such, can perhaps illuminate with the full vividness of contemporaneity a number of propositions advanced in the preceding paragraphs. I refer

[9] Cf. Ralph H. Turner, "The Real Self: From Institution to Impulse," *American Journal of Sociology* 81 (March 1976): 989–1016, in which Turner postulates two polar, often alternating sources of a person's self-concept: an institutional realm of more or less established values and norms and an impulsive realm of desire and discontent. Drawing on this suggestive theory, I would say that, whereas nostalgic self-imagery feeds upon desire and discontent it does so for the sake of refurbishing tarnished, institutionally accented versions of our "real selves."

to what in America today (and apparently to an extent in England and Europe as well)[10] has become a staple of social commentary in intellectual and lay circles alike, viz., why so much nostalgia *now*? Why the almost frenetic preoccupation of nearly every postpubescent age group with fads and fashions from the past, or, as the bemused woman in the William Hamilton cartoon remarks, "What do you suppose it means . . . when everything that's going on consists of stuff that's coming back?"[11] It would, of course, be difficult to establish "objectively" that the present era is any more nostalgic than previous ones, but the sense that it is so is as widespread as it is strong. So much so that jokes about nostalgia crop up in the media about as frequently as do nostalgia items themselves.

If it is not already evident on the basis of what has been said thus far, let it be stated with all due obviousness here: the nostalgia wave of the seventies is intimately related— indeed, the other side of the psychological coin, so to speak —to the massive identity dislocations of the sixties. Consider for a moment what America experienced during that decade[12] and one can begin to appreciate the appeal (and at some deeper level perhaps even the necessity) of the nostalgia wave that has followed in its wake. Quite apart from such specific traumas as the Vietnam war, the assassinations of the brothers Kennedy and of Martin Luther King, Jr., the ghetto riots, the student protests, the Civil Rights marches, the Kent State shooting, and so forth, millions upon millions of Americans experienced during those years what is perhaps

---

[10] See Michael Wood, "Nostalgia or Never: You Can't Go Home Again," *New Society*, November 7, 1974, pp. 343–346.

[11] *The New Yorker*, March 25, 1974, p. 42.

[12] The decade reference is of course somewhat arbitrary. Some of the "dislocations" like the Vietnam war and Watergate extended into the seventies just as some of the nostalgia revivals like the nineteen-thirties Busby Berkeley move musical and the wire-back soda chair can be traced back to the late nineteen-sixties.

the most wide-ranging, sustained and profound assault on native belief concerning the "natural" and "proper" that has ever been visited on a people over so short a span of time. To cite but a few of the more obvious "insults" made all the more proximate by their ceaseless exposure on television and in the other media: the outrageous notion that blacks are as good as whites and have a right to demand their rights forcefully despite local custom and past practice; the equally appalling notion that woman is man's equal and is not biologically destined to play the social roles or assume the expressive postures she had in the past; the repugnant claim that to be homosexual is neither criminal nor sick and that one can with legal impunity even go so far as to proclaim his or her "perversion" in public; the hippie's celebration of hallucinogenic drugs; the flower children's scornful disdain for the Protestant work ethic; the *Playboy* "philosophy" of a "screw is just a screw"; the apparent license—and, some would say active encouragement—of youth and other malcontents to disrespect and denigrate authority, be it a university president, a mayor, a president, or a pope; the civil liberterian and psychotherapeutic defense of obscenity and pornography along with the aggravated flouting by Hollywood and Main Street of the belief that "you don't talk dirty in public"; the legalization of abortion; the decriminalization of marijuana . . . and so forth.

Without expanding the catalogue of social affronts to absurd length, it should by now be evident that rarely in modern history has the common man had his fundamental, taken-for-granted convictions about man, woman, habits, manners, law, society, and God—entities of tremendous existential salience everywhere—so challenged, disrupted, and shaken. Clearly, if one can speak of a *collective* identity crisis, of a period of radical discontinuity in a people's sense of who and what they are, the late sixties and early seventies in America come as close to that condition as can be imagined. For millions it did indeed seem, although not necessarily to the point of absolute despair and disillusionment, that the center would no longer hold, that all certainties had been rendered problematic and that a rash of moral madness had broken upon the world.

In line then with our theory that the sources of nostalgic sentiment are to be found in felt threats to continuity of identity, what more fertile psychological ground than this for the sprouting of the lavish nostalgia crop of the nineteen-seventies? The current nostalgia wave offers, as many a social critic has noted, a retreat, a haven, an oasis, if you will, from the anxieties vast numbers felt (and continue to feel) about proposed alterations in mores and custom. And these alterations were not merely proposed; often they were enacted aggressively with all due media publicity, by one and another aggrieved minority that had until then suffered and chafed under the established scheme of things. The very profusion and variety of nostalgia styles and fads, one succeeding the other with even greater rapidity than women's fashions (this month the movie mania of the thirties, the next the drive-in automobile pubescence of the fifties, the next after that the bobbed hair, bell-bottomed abandon of the twenties—is a measure of how deep and wide-ranging (spanning more than a single age, class or subculture) the identity disturbances of the recent era have been.[13] Nostalgia became, in short, the means for holding onto and reaffirming identities which had been badly bruised by the turmoil of the times. In the "collective search for identity"[14] which is the hall-

---

[13] The nostalgic recourse was no doubt furthered to an extent by the symbolic license given it through the coincidence of the nation's bicentennial in 1976. I would argue, however, that this was at most a marginal influence, in no way as determinative as the identity dislocations of the sixties and early seventies.

[14] In the generally excellent, wide-arching book by that name Klapp, in his fascination with the apocalyptic, chiliastic, and utopian, tends to overlook more passive and backward-looking varieties of collective identity search. Collective nostalgia of the type discussed here eminently qualifies as such. See Orrin E. Klapp, *Col-*

mark of this postindustrial epoch—a search that in its constant soul-churning extrudes a thousand different fashions, ecstasies, salvations, and utopias—nostalgia looks backward rather than forward, for the familiar rather than the novel, for certainty rather than discovery.

Nostalgia, Politics, and Conservatism

Seen from this vantage point nostalgia is, of course, not without its political ramifications, although they, may not be quite what critics of the radical left say they are. Typically, liberals and radicals, as I had reason to note earlier, are disdainful of nostalgia movements, denouncing them as a fatuous form of collective self-indulgence at best and, at worst, a deliberately created, cleverly exploited obstacle on the path to reform or revolution, a somewhat diluted, yet still numbing, "opiate of the people." Some sense of the radical's irritation with nostalgic sentiment, even when confined to largely intellectual and specialist matters, is conveyed by the critic Christopher Lasch in his review of the book *The Making of the Modern Family* by Edward Shorter:

> It is time that historians of the family outgrew their infatuation with the concepts and methodology imported from social science and their own illusions about history. . . . Forgetting everything they learned as "conventional" historians they have made the transition from "traditional" to "modern" society into an all-purpose principle of historic explanation. Their insistence on the "fit" between the nuclear family and modernity satisfies the need to believe in historical progress, while their covert tendency to romanticize "the world we have lost" . . . even as they ostensibly glorify the one that replaced it, satisfies the current taste for nostalgia.[15]

A kinder, though still somewhat condescending, critical note

_____

lective Search for Identity (New York: Holt, Rinehart & Winston, 1969).

[15] *New York Review of Books*, December 11, 1975, p. 51.

is struck by the theologian Martin E. Marty as he seeks to distinguish nostalgia from other more serious uses of the past:

> But today's nostalgia is at worst bittersweet, at least designed to bring some pleasure. Our fashions, decor, and happenings evoke the thirties without the Depression, the forties sans the war, the fifties minus McCarthyism. These harmless activities deserve no monopoly on the past.[16]

These, like so many of the other observations of radical and liberal critics cited earlier in the chapter, carp at collective manifestations of nostalgia (and sometimes at more purely personal manifestations of it as well) for being conservative, if not outright reactionary, for turning peoples' heads away from the "important issues of the day" and incapacitating them for the sustained political action with which to correct the ills and undo the injustices of society. In Marxian terminology it is a subspecies of false consciousness, moreover, a particularly insidious subspecies in that it does not merely serve to obscure further an awareness of class struggle but, in defiance of the logic of historical dialectics, looks longingly backward to obsolete societal arrangements rather than forward to the better ones destined to emerge. Indeed, what more powerful antidote to revolutionary fervor than nostalgia's penchant for believing that the future can only be worse than the past?

All of this may of course be true, notwithstanding the unusual difficulty a historian or sociologist would have in tracing through the long-term political consequences of a particular nostalgia fad or movement or a spate of them as we are now witnessing. At the same time, before liberals and radicals succumb to excessive grimness over the matter it should be pointed out that nostalgia's conservative leaning is qualitatively different from the other ways in which conservatism and reaction manifest themselves. It is, even at the

[16] *New York Times,* February 6, 1975.

collective level, a good deal more passive, less strident, more inward, and, to be sure, more ephemeral. As was suggested in the previous section, it defuses what could be a powerful, panic-prone reactivity to jarring change and uncertainty by turning it into tender musing and mutually appreciative self-regard over a shared past. To the extent that constant change, at all levels and in all realms of social life, seems to be endemic to modern civilization, some such "outlet" or "safety valve" may be required. As suggested earlier, this allows time for needed change to be assimilated while giving the appearance, as nostalgia does, of meaningful links to the past. Would that Germany before Hitler or the United States before Senator Joseph R. McCarthy had responded with nostalgia's conservatism rather than the more virulent forms that gripped them as each struggled with the jarring social changes wrought by a great war. Indeed, when the threat of change appears *too* dire and *too* imminent, as seems to have been the case in Germany during the twenties and in the United States in the late forties and early fifties, the chance for nostalgic displacement is probably aborted as more extreme forms of mass reactivity lurch to the fore.

Nostalgia is more a crepuscular emotion. It takes hold when the dark of impending change is seen to be encroaching, although not *so* fast as to make a monster loom where but a moment ago stood a coat tree. In this sense, collective nostalgia represents a kind of inversion of Harold Lasswell's famous definition of politics as "the displacement of private affect onto public objects." In opposite fashion, nostalgia fads, fashions, and movements drain some of the negative affect and vague discontent generated by identity-jarring change in the public sphere (matters that could well be made the subject of considerable political conflict, as of course they sometimes are) and rechannels them into a more private sphere of shared memories and self-congratulatory sentiment over "the ways things were" and how those who came later made them "go wrong."

Nostalgia and the Generation of Generations

In this process of collective displacement nostalgia does something more as well. It mediates the selection, distillation, refinement, and integration of those scenes, events, personalities, attitudes, and practices from the past that make an identifiable *generation* of what would otherwise remain a featureless demographic cohort, e.g., the Edwardians, the jazz age generation, the children of the Depression, the silent generation, and the turned-on generation. However inexact and overlapping these designations are from a strictly chronological standpoint—and who in the end is to say when an era "really" began or came to an end?[17]—they nevertheless comprise the symbolic stuff from which a people's living sense of history is made. In this manner nostalgic sentiment, particularly its more reflexive variants, cultivates a sense of history. Through a kind of unwitting methodology it causes some persons to scrutinize its usually rash propositions concerning the superiority of things past and through such scrutiny to arrive at a more processual view of how the present came to differ from the past.[18] And while the resultant historical rendering may yet attribute greater virtue to the past, it will not do so as callously or mindlessly.

But prior to this, well before questions of the *writing* of a history arise, it is apparent that from the vantage of everyday life nostalgia-filtered memories give substance, shape, and significance to what, without them, would seem to contemporaries like the terrible adventitiousness of mere

---

[17] Of course, this is in part the business of the social historian. But since time is a river that flows continuously, the social historian must for the purposes of the story he or she wishes to tell be in the end as arbitrary as the layman in fixing the beginnings and endings of an era or generation.

[18] Whether this unwitting methodology can be brought into consciousness in a manner designed to purposefully further the historical enterprise is a question better left to historiographers and philosophers of history.

chronology. That is to say, the generation-generating memories bestow meaning and purpose on the otherwise accidental fact that contemporaries have seen, thought, and felt many of the same things at much the same time. At least in imagination, this infuses our relationship with distant and unknown contemporaries with some of that feeling of togetherness that Schutz reserves for "consociates," persons with whom we do not merely coexist but with whom we also have a "We-Relationship."[19] Particularly in societies that are strongly age-graded like our own, nostalgic memory helps foster a feeling of kind within an age group which, temporarily at least, can transcend divisions of class, race, religion, and region. This is particularly apparent on national holidays and other commemorative occasions when like-aged persons are led to reminisce on "how things were then" and "how they've changed."

Of course, the collective processes of communication by which an age cohort forges a generational identity for itself are probably immensely complex as well as elusive[20] A plethora of questions come at once to mind, almost none of which can be answered adequately as yet. For example:

1. Is the nostalgia that is induced by widespread (though at first probably mute and private) fears of change, the sole or even principal triggering mechanism of the generation-defining process? Do other memory-related psychic states—for example, repression, reminiscence, simple affectless recall—play a part in the genesis of the process?

2. Is there at the collective level some underlying generation-defining "impulse," as it were, which would exert itself irrespective of whether the discontinuities of history afforded maturing age groups reason to wax nostalgic over

---

[19] Alfred Schutz, *Collected Papers, Volume I,* (The Hague: Martinus Nijhoff, 1962), pp. 15–17.

[20] Some highly suggestive observations along these lines are to be found in Anselm Strauss *Mirrors and Masks* (Glencoe, Ill.: Free Press, 1959), Chaps. V and VI.

their pasts? In other words, is there, above and beyond history as such, some unquenchable need or inescapable structural constraint for "inventing" generations?

The weight of our argument thus far would suggest that generations are invented *because* of events, not in spite of them. There is however the arresting fact that the commonly identifiable American generations of recent times all evidence a symbolic span of approximately ten years: the lost generation (1919-1929), from the end of World War I to the 1929 stock market crash; the children of the Depression (1930-1941), from the crash to America's entrance into World War II; the forties war and the Cold War generation (1941-1952), the war and immediate postwar years to the election of President Eisenhower; the Silent Generation (1953-1963), the Eisenhower years of relative calm and affluence up to the assassination of President Kennedy; the Protest (Rebel or Turned-On) Generation,[21] the sixties' turmoils up to roughly America's withdrawal from Vietnam and Nixon's resignation over Watergate. The ten-year intervals over this limited span of historical time may, of course, be purely coincidental, although they also suggest a certain inherent periodicity in the generation-defining phenomenon. At any rate, it is probably of greater significance that despite their approximately equal duration the intervals are bracketed in collective memory by major historical events rather than by simple chronological references *per se*.

[21] It is probably still too early in the generation-defining process for a fixed generational designation to have crystallized for those who reached adulthood during this period. One sees here, as one would in the early definitional stages of almost any collective movement, a certain amount of rivalry and competition among symbols. Which will emerge ultimately as the defining one for this generation depends probably on the character of the historic shocks and discontinuities it has yet to experience, possibly in the nineteen-eighties or nineties. Then the cohort that came of age in the sixties and early seventies will probably gravitate toward that symbol of their past which most vividly throws into relief their current experience.

3. Inasmuch as the anxieties and discontents induced by a cataclysmic event or abrupt social change are experienced (and often only subliminally at that) by *individuals,* each necessarily from the limited vantage point of his or her own distinctive biography, how are these revealed, exchanged, and shared among a people so as to lay the groundwork for a *collective* nostalgic response? (How, for example, do contemporary, conventionally brought up males of middling years express and communicate among themselves the anxiety and disillusionment many must feel over their sexual status vis-à-vis the new, more liberated role stances of women?) Is group discussion or private confession the favored forum for such agonizing; and if, as seems likely, both are involved, by what process does the privately felt fear or discontent come to be viewed as part of the common condition?[22] Humor and satire, we know, often function in this manner, although it would seem that still other social forms like collective nostalgia serve much the same purpose.

4. The psychological ground having been laid for some collective nostalgic response, why from the immense aggregate of events, celebrities, styles and practices from one's past that is available to an age cohort are some rather than others "chosen" as symbolic vehicles for defining and delineating a generation? Not only why, but—again—*how* is the process of symbol competition, elision and crystalization mediated among different circles, groups and publics whose members' other life interests must surely outweigh that coincident to their being of more or less the same age? How in the working out of this complex social process does the

---

[22] Collective behavior theory of the type developed by Robert Park, Herbert Blumer, and their students holds that it is on the basis of such vague, ill-defined dissatisfactions and discontents that fashion changes, crazes, and other mass expressive movements come about. Nostalgia movements and fads should also be included in the class of phenomena wherein vague private discontents find expression in some common public symbol. See Herbert Blumer, "Collective Behavior," in A. M. Lee, ed., *New Outline of the Principles of Sociology* (New YOrk: Barnes & Noble, 1946), pp. 216–218.

past reality (as it was experienced then) come in collective memory to be simplified, romanticized, or otherwise distoted? Bartlett in his famous work of a half-century ago suggests that processes which parallel precisely those of individual recall must obtain for collective memory as well.[23] But this has never been demonstrated.

5. Finally, and of rather obvious relevance, what part do intellectuals, artists and the mass media play in all of the above, that is, in the discovery, construction, and diffusion of generational objects of nostalgia? Clearly these groups are deeply implicated, and while it is not possible to treat the topic at length here we shall have some things to say about it in the chapter on "Contemporary Nostalgia" that follows.

But whatever the fine details of the processes responsible for collective nostalgia—and the above questions are designed to at least point to some of them—it should be kept in mind that nostalgic sentiment dwells as the very heart of a generation's identity; that without it, it is unlikely that a "generation" could come to conceive of itself as such or that "generations" in advance or arrears of it would accede to the distinctive historical identity it claims for itself. And, in large part it is because human consciousness can forge "generations" from the raw materials of history that the generations come to speak to each other, as it were, each reminding the other of "precious things" about to be lost or forgotten. Thus, the dialogue of history is itself enriched and given dramatic form far beyond that which could be evoked from a mere chronology of places, persons, and events.

Conclusion

Generational nostalgic sentiment, therefore, creates as it conserves. It creates because the past is never something simply there just waiting to be discovered. Rather, the

[23] F. C. Bartlett, *Remembering* (Cambridge, England: Cambridge University Press, 1932), p. 309.

remembered past like all other products of human consciousness is something that must constantly be filtered, selected,
arranged, constructed, and reconstructed from collective
experience. And the fulcrum for this great labor can only be
the present with its shared anxieties, aspirations, hopes,
fears, and fantasies. But still, the nostalgic creation is, as I
have tried to suggest from a number of different vantage
points, a special kind of creation, one powerfully permeated
in feeling and thought by a conviction of the essential superiority of what was over what is or appears destined to be.
Hence the associated impulse to conserve and recover.

In this manner nostalgic sentiment partakes of one of the
great dialectical processes of Western civilization: the ceaseless tension of change vs. stability, innovation vs. reaffirma-
tion, new vs. old, utopia vs. the golden age. Its role in this
dialectic is that of a brake on the headlong plunge into the
future; a rather tenuous brake, to be sure, since little in
contemporary life seems capable of arresting the march of
modern technology and rational organization. Nonetheless
it is, perhaps, enough of a brake to cause some individuals
and peoples to look before they knowingly leap.

At least since the Enlightenment insistent and often strident demands have gnawed at the soul of Western man,
demands for change, self-improvement, more efficient
organization, modernization, uplift, reform and reconstitution—all those attributes that are in accord with the doctrine
of man's almost infinite plasticity and perfectability and that
converge finally in the idea of Progress as it was propounded
and analyzed by the historian J. B. Bury.[24] Nostalgia fosters
a kind of primitive resistance to such urgings, to the probing
and poking, to that close examination and magnification
which in the view of Max Weber has made for the disenchantment of the world. Nostalgia reenchants, if only for a while
until the inexorable processes of historical change exhaust
that past which offered momentary shelter from a worrisome
but finally inexorable future.

[24] J. B. Bury, *The Idea of Progress* (London: Macmillan, 1920).

Where were you in 1962?

*1973 advertisement for the
film* American Graffiti

"Nostalgia—it just ain't what it used to be."

*Attributed to the novelist
Peter de Vries by Bert
Prelutsky,* Los Angeles
Times, *Calendar Section,
June 25, 1977*

*Remember Nostalgia? Remember when you remem-
bered tha 1950s? Remember when you remem-
bered the '60s? Well it's all back. . . . Yes, you remembered it all in the '70s, the Golden Age of Nostalgia.
And now, for the first time—the only time, the last
time before it's all exported—Bobby Bison, the King
of Nostalgia, is making available selections from your
own personal memory!*

*George W. S. Trow, "Bobby
Bison's Big Memory Offer,"*
The New Yorker, *June 30,
1974, p. 27*

6

CONTEMPORARY NOSTALGIA

PERHAPS THE FIRST AND MOST OBVIOUS thing to note about contemporary nostalgia is that it is very big business. Quite apart from the movies, TV, and other popular media, which are constantly churning out a tremendous variety of nostalgia "products" harking back as far as the twenties (probably the oldest live memory bank for which a commercially large enough audience can still be found), thousands of firms exist dedicated to preserving, propagating, and deriving income from some slice of the recent past about which people feel or can be made to feel nostalgic. Thus, for example, *Liberty Magazine,* which in its original format went out of business in the early nineteen-forties, appears again in 1972 as a quarterly devoted solely to the verbatim reprinting of articles that appeared in its pages during the twenties and thirties on such movie and radio celebrities as Charlie Chaplin, Fred Allen, Fanny Brice, and Fibber McGee and Molly. Under an exact reproduction of its original logotype it now designates itself *The Nostalgia Magazine.* Even the very "trendy" magazine *New West,* in a September

1977 issue, features a profile of Marilyn Monroe "if she were alive today at age 52." A mail order firm drawing on the extensive list of American Express credit card holders advertises for $60.00 a slightly scaled down facsimile of the famous thirties Philco Baby Grand table model radio.(Shying away, however, from what some may regard as an excess of verisimilitude, the advertiser assures prospective buyers that this "circa 1932" replica is replete with "solid state AM/FM receiver with AVC and variable tone control.") For a one-dollar membership fee the Nostalgia Book Club of New Rochelle, N.Y., promises, along with a free book on the life of Judy Garland and the club's bulletin, *Reminiscing Time,* "personal service—just like 1939. No computers." Radio Yesteryear of Croton-on-Hudson, N.Y., offers long-playing records at $5.95 each of swing band broadcasts, comedy shows, and daytime serials from the nineteen-thirties and forties:

> You probably have trouble remembering that TV show you watched last Tuesday. Yet you'll remember Jack Benny, Little Orphan Annie and The Shadow as long as you live. Why? Maybe the reason is that Radio put your imagination to work. The sets, the props and the costumes were all in your head.

The LP records and eight-track cartridges of the shows have, naturally, been rechanneled for stereo sound and can be purchased through the mail via credit card. Aging baseball fans can with the help of Sports Nostalgia, Inc., of Upper Saddle River, N.J., rekindle joyful boyhood days by reacquiring, at premium prices, the picture trading cards of famous ballplayers which they probably threw away when on reaching adolescence their interest first turned to girls.

No account of the American nostalgia industry, however, can overlook those veritable national shrines to past pleasures and beauties—with just enough contemporaneity thrown in to make them sanitary, efficient, and immensely profitable— the California Disneyland and Florida Disney World. (That

I'M CONSUMED BY NOSTALGIA.

NOT FOR MY CHILDHOOD BUT FOR ANDY HARDY'S CHILDHOOD.

2-19 ©1978 JULES FEIFFER

NOT FOR MY PARENTS BUT FOR LEWIS STONE AND FAY HOLDEN AS MY PARENTS.

NOT FOR MY OLD GIRL FRIENDS BUT FOR JUDY GARLAND AND ANN RUTHERFORD AS MY GIRL FRIENDS.

NOT FOR THE BRONX BUT FOR #1 SHADY LANE, JUST OFF MAIN STREET, SMALLVILLE, U.S.A.

I DON'T PINE FOR MY REAL PAST.

I PINE FOR MY MGM PAST.

FOR FIELD NEWSPAPER SYNDICATE, 1978

these least "traditional" of states should provide the sites for such massive nostalgic shrines suggests anew, symbolically and by indirection, how much the sources of collective nostalgia are to be found in the present and not the past.) Here, not only are visitors reimmersed through almost every mimetic device known to man in memories of the famous Disney animated cartoon characters whom they came to know, and perhaps love, as children, but they are led back sentimentally to the small-town atmosphere of America at the turn of the century. That few of us are old enough to have experienced those days at first hand is of little account. So successful have Disney and the other myth-makers of the mass media been in celebrating and memorializing this "age of innocence" in the American imagination that, even though we may not have lived then, we feel—because of the movies we have seen, the stories we have read, the radio serials we've listened to—"as if we had." This, incidentally, is a nice, if rare, instance of a created, secondhand reality (a romanticized *version* of a slightly earlier historical reality) practically acquiring the same nostalgic status as something experienced firsthand in our very own lives. Of course, the transpositional process is facilitated in large part by the circumstance that the "turn of the century" is not so *far* removed or discontinuous in historical time as to make it altogether inaccessible to contemporary sensibilities. The Disney reconstruction of that period acquires, despite considerable historical inauthenticity, a certain subjective credibility by virtue of the reminiscences we have heard from parents and grandparents, the popular songs of the period that are still sung (e.g., "When You Were Sweet Sixteen," "Shine On Harvest Moon," "I Wonder Who's Kissing Her Now"), and the not altogether quaint photographs we still see of city streets with their trolley lines, gaslights, and men in bowler hats standing about looking slightly startled. Thus, much survives well into the present from the turn of the century that is visually and evocatively recognizable in a way that, for example, the Civil War photographs of Matthew Brady, the prints of Daumier, or the late eighteenth-/early nineteenth-century etchings of town squares with their neat baroque symmetries and elegant Italianate orthography are not recognizable any longer.

But even in so vast a memory emporium as Disneyland the nostalgic investment in the putatively wholesome and simple qualities of American small-town life circa 1900 is dwarfed by the near worshipful attention lavished on the characters, plots, scenes, and events from Walt Disney's own animated cartoons and feature films. And this, perhaps, is a clue to what is most striking and interesting about contemporary nostalgia, namely, that not only is it propagated on a vast scale by the mass media but the very objects of collective nostalgia are in themselves media creations from the recent past. In other words, in their ceaseless search for new marketable objects of nostalgia the media now do little but devour themselves. Or, as a cynic might put it, nostalgia exists of the media, by the media, and for the media. It is to the vicissitudes and implications of this phenomenon that I am about to turn.

First, however, it is important to distinguish between *collective* nostalgia and what for want of a better term I call *private* nostalgia. This distinction has much more to do with the symbolic and imaginary *content* of nostalgia than with nostalgic experience itself. Whether we conceive of nostalgia as an emotion or as a form of consciousness (and in this book I have viewed it as both), the subjective experience remains much the same irrespective of whether its objects are of a collective or of a more private character. Both display the same yearning and adoration for some slice of a personally experienced past. Collective nostalgia, however, refers to that condition in which the symbolic objects are of a highly public, widely shared, and familiar character, those symbolic resources from the past that under proper conditions can trigger wave upon wave of nostalgic feeling in millions of persons at the same time. Collective symbols of this type can of course range from the most awesome (e.g., the Allies' liberation of Paris from the Germans in 1944) to the most trivial (e.g., Harpo Marx's capacious cloak with its warehouse of food, tools, and assorted bric-a-brac).

By contrast, *private* nostalgia refers to those symbolic images and allusions from the past that by virtue of their source in a particular person's biography tend to be more idiosyncratic, individuated, and particularistic in their reference, e.g., the memory of a parent's smile, the garden view from a certain window of a house once lived in, for Proust the little cakes from his childhood at Combray. This, of course, is not to say that another human is incapable of appreciating or even identifying vicariously with the *general* process by which such past private experience is converted into nostalgic sentiment. The social interaction that sustains culture (along with a common humanity) does, after all, instill in us those experiential categories by which we can know what another must *in general* be feeling without knowing the particulars from his past that cause him to feel that way.[1] For him, however, the particularities remain important and in large part constitute the basis of his distinctive identity as an *individual*. Even were he eager to share them with us, in the end they cannot make the same exquisite impress on us as they do on him. Hence the need to retain some kind of a distinction between collective symbols that can be widely shared by many and more private ones whose contents are known only to the individual and, perhaps, a few of his intimates.

But having made the distinction it must also be conceded that *too* sharp a line between them cannot be drawn. Since both fall essentially within the realm of subjective experi-

---

[1] This view parallels closely Mead's "generalized other" except that it refers to the subjective generalizability of experiential categories rather than to role-taking *per se*. George H. Mead, *Mind, Self and Society* (Chicago: University of Chicago Press, 1934), pp. 152–164.

ence, it is likely that, except for the poles of the public-private contimuum (e.g., a presidential figure at one end, Proust's madeleines at the other), there is in most of us much overlapping, interweaving, and transmutation of nostalgia's symbolic materials at every level of subjective generality and specificity. Thus, a nostalgic summoning of "everybody's favorite song from 1943" (essentially a collectively oriented symbol) may inwardly shade off into some very private reminiscences of a particular romance in a particular place on a particular day, replete with special fragrances, sounds, and visual traces. Conversely, the nostalgic recall of a favorite friend's facial expression and speech mannerism may be suffused with equally evocative memories of the era's clothing fashions, popular diversions, and political happenings (e.g., the Army–McCarthy hearings, the protest marches of the sixties). To which category then are these experiences to be assigned, the collective or the private? Obviously in some part to both, the exact separation having finally less to do with the quality of the actual subjective experience *per se* than with the purposes for which we are examining it. In the end, therefore, it is probably best to conceive of a rather seamless symbolic web linking collective and private nostalgia. This is a web whose segments could be differentiated and distinguished if need be, but only if it is first recognized that the need to distinguish and differentiate resides more in the mind of the analyst than in the phenomenon itself.

Nostalgia, Past and Present

Even if we knew something more than we do of the history of collective nostalgia in this country, the very amorphousness of the phenomenon would make it exceedingly difficult to sketch its changing topography, so to speak—what its principal memory objects have been. How widely shared, by what population groups? How frequently and quickly one collective nostalgia complex (e.g., an adoration of the Jazz Age) has been displaced by another (e.g., memories of the solidarity of the war years)? Whether in general some eras—for example, the present—have been more nostalgia-prone than other? What all of this has meant for the political life of the country? For the arts? For the sense of hope or despair with which a people live?

These unanswered, or at best poorly answered, questions notwithstanding, there is a distinct conviction among numerous cultural critics and commentators, this writer included, that as the aphorism would have it "nostalgia ain't what it used to be." And if there is truth to this intriguingly reflexive witticism, it is to be traced, I would say, to the following circumstances:

1. Whereas previously the landscape of collective nostalgia was inhabited mainly by persons, places, and events of a political or civic character, today it is inhabited increasingly and perhaps even predominantly by media creations, personalities, and allusions. In other words, where there once dwelt presidents, proclamations, and civic achievements of some sort (e.g., the opening of the Golden Gate Bridge, the bank moratorium of 1933), there now dwell media celebrities, old movies, TV shows, popular music styles, and dated speech mannerisms. Not that the first have been completely obliterated or that the second have become ubiquitous, but the critical mix or balance has shifted markedly toward the second. Moreover, even the *public* event or personage, when we bring it to nostalgic memory, is now more and more mediated through a distinctive *media* filter or stamp, e.g., the voice of Franklin Roosevelt *over* radio delivering his fireside chats, the hysterical excitement of Herbert Morrison, a *radio announcer, describing* the explosion of the Hindenburg dirigible at Lakehurst, N.J., in 1937, Ed Murrow's *radio voice reporting* the London blitz of 1941, the *TV cameras capturing* the gunning down of Lee Harvey Oswald by Jack Ruby in the Dallas courthouse in 1963.

125

2. Because there is money to made from nostalgia the media have come to devour their past creations at an ever increasing rate. A consequence has been that the time span between the "original appearance," as it were, and its nostalgic recycling has shrunk to a fraction of what it once was. Oddly, the recent past is made to seem as a result more removed and historic than previous ways of subjectively relating to it would have made it appear. (Perhaps by now we can nostalgically remember doubting in 1973 whether one could feel nostalgia for what had happened as recently as 1962, as the advertisements for the film *American Graffiti* were inviting us to do.) Or, as more than one comedian or cartoonist is bound to have observed, by tomorrow yesterday will be ancient history, it's today that's nostalgia. This, too, has possibly contributed to the sense of constant change, disappearance, and discontinuity which so many moderns, laymen and social commentators alike, complain of. If what was in time so recent can be made to appear so remote, is anything permanent? Are our families, spouses, and friends vulnerable to the same quick nostalgic recasting and discarding of their being as are yesterday's media stars and celebrities?

3. Even what passes for the private and intimate in our nostalgic memory—sunsets, birthdays, family gatherings, friends, and lovers—has because of the pervasiveness of the mass media in our lives acquired a more common, familiar, and transferable quality. This has also served to blur and possibly confound what once was a fairly well-drawn interior division between the private and the public. In contrast to that time before the media came to reveal "all," one soon realizes now that the private, including even that which can be viewed as shameful or disreputable, is not nearly as singular or insular as had been imagined. Moreover, as many who have come out of the closet have discovered, nowadays the opening of the private to public view can be a good deal less painful than had once been feared. On the contrary, the act of exposure seems, as often as not, to draw a measure of

126

acclaim. In any event, the media confessional mode has become increasingly commonplace, and it has in turn served to relax the guardedness once assumed toward one's "most private" memories.

These three circumstances—collective nostalgia's drift to media products, the ever greater speed with which this happens, and the rearrangement of the spheres of private and public memories—are obviously not unrelated. Economically and culturally they function to reinforce each other. In searching out reasons why one or the other has come into being perhaps all three can be treated as a piece.

The most obvious reason for collective nostalgia's monopolization by and through the mass media is that the media, particularly since the advent of movies and radio, have come to play a far more prominent part in our mental lives than could possibly have been the case in the pre-mass communications era. This is not to say, as some simple-minded critics charge, that we are wholly dominated by the mass media and are the abject slaves of their every whim and fancy. Rather, what can be said is that a great deal more of what we think, feel, and believe—our innermost images of the world around us and its happenings—originates with the media and is, moreover, processed and defined by them. Not only do they select the content of what is communicated to us, but they fix the manner in which it is presented to us as well. Thus, while one person may wax nostalgic over the late Elvis Presley's rock 'n' roll hip-twitching from the fifties and another may feel revulsion toward it, the fact that it was Elvis Presley, a movie-TV-record star, is known to practically everyone. This supplies an important point of common cultural reference in the media's subsequent nostalgic recycling of his image and in the collective memories that can be linked to him.

The prominence of mass media cultural products in our lives has, of course, been greatly accelerated in the modern era by the shortening of the work week and the commensurate increase in leisure time. Because more people have more time away from what Aristotle termed "necessitous labor" and because, as numerous surveys attest, vast numbers are not particularly inclined to pursue recreations of their own invention, the media along with mass spectator sports and commercial amusements since early in this century have produced and propagated cultural goods and services on a scale and with a rapidity formerly undreamed of.[2] And, as with consumer products generally, so with the mass media: the constant aim is to develop formats, characters, plots, images, allusions, genres, novelties, and celebrities of the greatest possible mass appeal. To succeed at this is the equivalent of that product standardization which makes for great economies of scale and profit maximization. This is not to say that the media always succeed in their aim or that competition among them is not frequently fierce. But, from the industry side at least, there is, despite an occasionally strong countertrend, an in-built structural tendency toward the concentration and homogenization of cultural products rather than their diversification and elaboration. Mass literacy and the advance of public education in the modern state have played no small part in these developments. Basically, these have served to lay the cognitive groundwork for that *common* culture upon which the media in their massiveness depend.

But it is not the prominence of the mass media alone that is responsible for the rearranging of the landscape of our memory. In addition, there is the parallel and not unrelated development of the decline of localisms and regionalisms, the progressive fostering of *national* cultures, and what Edward Shils has so aptly termed the "bringing into the center of society" of what were once numerous parochial and diverse groupings.[3] These processes, too, may act to deprive

[2] For an excellent discussion of these matters, see Sebastian de Grazia, *Of Time, Work and Leisure* (Garden City, N. Y.: Doubleday Anchor, 1964).

[3] Edward Shils, "Centre and Periphery," in *Selected Essays by Edward Shils* (Chicago: Center for Social Organization Studies, University of Chicago, 1970), pp. 1–14.

our nostalgias of certain of their more idiosyncratic, private, and individuated nuances. For, as was pointed out in the chapter on "Nostalgia and Identity," nostalgic emotion thrives on a perception of one's youthful past as having somehow been specially marked off and "different" from that of the "average" member of society. Strong local, regional, and ethnic traditions against the backdrop of a more uniform national culture will often inspire and sustain such a perception, especially where people have drifted some, though not completely, from their parochial origins. In any case, the gradual disappearance of much that was locally and regionally distinctive in America, as well as in other modern societies, is destined to promote a certain homogeneity in the collective coffers of nostalgic memory.

Closely interwoven with the rise of the mass media and the passing of localisms there remains, of course, the greatly stepped-up geographic, occupational, and social mobility which vast numbers of persons, Americans in particular, experience in the course of their lives. To move many times in one's youth and to change neighborhoods and friends every few years can only mean that a relatively permanent *home* in a specific geographic locale with its own distinctive atmosphere—the classic stuff of nostalgia—can no longer shape memory to nearly the extent it once did. Here too, nostalgic reverie loses some of the biographically distinctive moorings it once fastened on so naturally. Instead, media products may now serve memory where once houses, streets, and persons did.

Distinctive Features of Media-Dominated Nostalgia

But as I have argued, all this does not mean that "nostalgia is dead" or that its emotional texture has altered markedly. On the contrary, given the sheer rate of social change in the modern world and the resultant profound identity changes, it is quite possible that nostalgia is more "alive" and more deeply felt than ever. What I have tried to establish is that for ever greater numbers of persons in the mass society the *objects* of nostalgia's exercise have changed, but not the exercise itself. To offer at the risk of a certain redundancy an additional example: whereas once the nostalgic reminiscence of, let us say, a thirty-five-year-old was likely to turn to memories of the wide-porched house on Elm Street, the escapades of the gang of kids on the block, and the warm dinner gatherings of family and in-laws on Sunday afternoons, today it is more likely to fix on old TV shows, dancing to rock 'n' roll records, and such popular fads of the period as hula hoops and trampolines. What is significant about this alteration is the changed symbolic context of the respective materials of memory brought to mind, not the felt quality of the emotion *per se*. Because they are commercially produced and distributed *en masse,* the media images tend toward a much greater uniformity of meaning and constriction of evocative association. Their possibilities for subsequent recycling, manipulation, and symbolic control are, therefore, greatly enhanced. All else being equal, media-derived objects of nostalgia, poignant though they may be in their own right, probably do not admit of quite the same diversity of reference and individuality of association as do more private objects of memory generated in more private settings. By the very circumstances of their creation and the largely commercial vicissitudes of their subsequent diffusion, mass media creations have to be of a more public, negotiable, and symbolically homogeneous character.

This is not to say that one does not have intensely private associations as well to what are essentially public media images from the past. He who was a city dweller in the nineteen-thirties may, for example, associate the memory of Jack Benny's whining Sunday evening voice with the sound of an elevated train passing nearby while the person from a small town might more likely associate it with the swoosh of lawn sprinklers and the chatter of katydids. But that it is

Jack Benny's whining voice from many years ago, a voice fondly remembered by millions, which is triggering these secondary nostalgic associations in each is by no means an insignificant cultural datum. For in that whine there also dwell common memories of the Depression, the allure of a Hollywood society (cocktail parties, chauffeurs, and country clubs) that most Americans could only dimly apprehend, and gentle admonitions on the pitfalls of penny-pinching and the traps of planning one's daily life too carefully. In this kind of nostalgic configuration—and so much contemporary nostalgia is of this order—it is the movie, radio, or TV image from the past that locates the common background experience, the gestalt *ground* as it were. The more private, peripheral associations to elevated trains or lawn sprinklers, while "part of the picture," do not join in memory the experiential ground that is common to both parties.

Because the popular media have come increasingly to serve as their own repository for the nostalgic use of the past, they may also have helped further what many observers see as the ever greater symbolic unity of American society and, for that matter, of postindustrial Western society generally. That is, the media through the sheer massiveness and pervasiveness of their popular appeal fulfill a culturally assimilationist, nationalizing function which patriotic exhortation and pluralistic politics before them could not accomplish.[4] *E pluribus unum* is to be found in things besides money and

[4] This, of course, runs side by side with the previously discussed decline of localism and regionalism in modern societies, a claim that may seem to fly in the face of the emergence in recent years of such regional secessionist movements as the Scottish, Welsh, Basque, Catalonian, Flemish, and Breton. By and large, however, I would suggest that these movements are in part a kind of last-ditch attempt to hold onto and revivify a vanishing regional culture as much as they are expressions of vital, still genuine continuities with a regional past. We might note here that in its own right this condition lends itself to the almost studied cultivation of regionalist and folklorist nostalgias, a topic touched on earlier in the book.

constitutions. In proffering the personalities, plots, and styles from five, ten, and twenty-five years ago to feed our nostalgic reverie, the media not only bring many millions of us together in mind and time but also fashion for us the color and contour of much of our intersubjective culture. When recalling the thirties, millions of older Americans are likely, first off and without coaching, to think of the Sunday evening comedy shows on radio and of the MGM galaxy of movie stars. Recalling the forties, somewhat younger Americans are likely to remember the Andrews sisters and the recordings of the big swing bands. Those in their teens in the nineteen-fifties are likely to call forth memories of Presley, rock 'n' roll and the erotic audacity of the Twist. And, naturally, these objects of nostalgic imagery do not merely drift about aimlessly and emptily in our hearts and minds; they are as umbrellas for a host of more private nostalgic memories of persons, places, and happenings in our lives— a love affair, a beautiful vacation, an inspiring teacher, a favorite aunt, *et cetera* and *ad infinitum*. But it is the media that gather us under these ample symbolic unbrellas, and that is, I repeat, by no means an insignificant datum. At the very least, it is one whose cultural implications are worth probing, even if its exact relevance for the future of collective behavior in America cannot be fully ascertained at this remove.

Some Fanciful Possibilities and Their Problems

Because the media in general and the audio-visual media in particular can with such great facility nostalgically exploit their past cultural products for present pleasure and profit, is it too far-fetched to imagine that one day soon, if it has not already come to pass, the selection and promotion of media products will be guided as much by a concern for their future "nostalgia exploitation potential" (NEP, as the trade is likely to dub it) as for their immediate "hit" possibilities? In other words, will movie studios, TV networks, and record companies come to include among their staffs "nostalgia specialists" whose job will be to advise management on which shows, personalities, and genres stand the best chance for subsequent successful recycling, not merely once but several times over in the decades to follow? The advice may extend to such fairly subtle matters as how long after its first appearance a show or personality is to be nostalgically "rediscovered" (half a generation later? a whole one?) and the conditions that would prove most propitious for such a resurrection. And if this much can be anticipated and historically programmed in advance—although it is by no means certain that it can—might not the initial design of the media product seek somehow to maximize its future nostalgia potential? Thus, for example, one would make sure to include in the TV star's video personality some idiosyncrasy of speech, dress, or gesture that twenty years or so later would be capable of triggering in an audience a gush of (additional revenue-producing) nostalgic sentiment. In short, the potential for a delayed nostalgic reworking of current material may emerge as a much more conscious element in media product design than is presently the case. Rather than planned obsolescence, what may occur here could perhaps better be termed planned *revivification*.

From a purely commercial point of view, however, the ideal formula for the media would seem to be some minimax balance of both obsolescence and revivification potentials. Under such a formula a product would be permitted a decently short initial life so that the incremental economic stimulus deriving from the introduction of new products could be realized, that is, the planned obsolescence phase. This would be followed by successive nostalgia-borne halflives some fifteen, thirty, and perhaps forty years later—the planned revivification phase. Indeed, a case can be made that commercial American television is willy-nilly, if not neces-

133

sarily by rational design, already approximating this formula, as witness the many instantly popular though relatively short-lived new shows that appear with each new season along with new replays of old shows—e.g., *You Bet Your Life, The Honeymooners, I Love Lucy, Star Trek.* But since the mere revival of "old" hit shows seems insufficient to appease the current American hunger for nostalgia, onto the market has also come that strange hybrid form, the new-old show, shows that are "new" perhaps in the strict technical sense of not having been produced before but are so unabashedly permeated by qualities of genre revivalism as to make them appear authentic "leftovers" from an earlier era, e.g., *Happy Days, The Waltons, The Little House on the Prairie.*

Similarly, the movie industry, too, has sought to doubly exploit the nostalgia market by, on the one hand, merchandising such pastiche compendiums of earlier musicals and comedies as *That's Entertainment, That's Entertainment Part II,* and *The Golden Age of Comedy* and, on the other hand, producing "new" films in the genre-revival mold whose appeal is mainly nostalgic, e.g., *The Sting, Butch Cassidy and the Sundance Kid, Paper Moon, Hearts of the West* and, up to a point, even such "serious" films as *Bonnie and Clyde, They Shoot Horses, Don't They?, The Great Gatsby,* and *The Day of the Locust.*[5]

At minimum, therefore, it would seem that a lively awareness already exists among media people regarding the later nostalgia potential of much of their past and current output. In principle, at least, this now rather diffuse awareness could probably be rationalized and incorporated into the design of new material so as to maximize the chance that it would later be successfully recycled as nostalgia. This seemingly

[5] For some cogent observations on the enhanced capacity of the contemporary arts generally to utilize materials from their own past, see Leonard B. Meyer, *Music, the Arts and Ideas* (Chicago: University of Chicago Press, 1967), pp. 87–232.

paradoxical state of affairs of programming the old into the new nicely accords with the suggestive metaphor of Marshal McLuhan on the habit of modern media-ridden culture to travel into the future with an eye cocked on its rear-view mirror. The question remains however, whether the media, employing the most sophisticated market research, merchandising, and publicity techniques known to the trade, could so program, and in effect dictate, our future nostalgias. Despite the zeal the record and TV industries could be expected to devote to the project, is it even a near certainty, for example, that today's teenagers will feel, twelve to fifteen years hence, the same nostalgia for Elton John as teenagers from the sixties now feel for the Beatles? Were nostalgia wholly dependent on the intrinsic character of the remembered object alone, it could conceivably lend itself to this kind of future programming with all of the associated grim implications for mass manipulation. But is has been our thesis all along that nostalgia has much less to do with the past than with the present; it is present anxieties, concerns, and existential discontinuities that evoke and amplify it. Although once aroused it may well tend to gravitate toward some rather than other classes of remembered objects, the formal intrinsic properties of which can perhaps be specified to an extent. But this modicum of foreknowledge notwithstanding, it would be a serious error, as was pointed out earlier, to confuse what lends itself to nostalgic sentiment with what arouses it.

For the media to become absolute prestidigitators of our future nostalgia would require that they not only furnish us with the remembrances on which our nostalgia is to fasten—something I *do* believe they have come increasingly to do—but also control the times (i.e., events, happenings, and moods) that generate our nostalgia. And this is something that even they in their most narcissistic moments of self-adulation cannot remotely pretend to be capable of doing.

Doubtless there are some of Orwellian temper who, holding to the solipsism that the times are what the media say they are, fear that the media will be at some point in the near future, if not already, capable of completely forming and manipulating our sense of the times. Thus, for example, if one wanted to cultivate "in the masses" a protracted nostalgic mood following a period of "regulated turmoil,"[6] one would have to instill via the media a sense of resignation and relative quiescence.

Such visions of absolute control, particularly over matters of subjective disposition and collective mood, must for now, however, be relegated to the science fiction rantings of some megalomaniacal minister of propaganda. History has shown repeatedly that there are simply too many wrong turns, inadvertencies, unanticipated developments, holocausts, and catastrophes to permit so fine a degree of prediction and control. And, while advance techniques of communication, record-keeping, and information processing may reduce the unknowns and uncertainties to a considerable extent, this still would fall far short of the authoritarian omniscience and omnipotence required to produce the "desired" collective behaviors in a populace. Besides, the very calculus of such thinking presumes an absolute monopoly by a single person or group over the means of public communication, something that can be conceived of only in the instance of totalitarian

[6] The early days of the nineteen-sixties Cultural Revolution in China had some of this quality of planned psychological manipulation, but even there matters got out of hand. More by way of revolutionary fervor was unleashed by Mao and his circle than appears to have been intended. And, whether the current, transparently manipulative attempts to dampen zealotry by reintroducing elements of tradition, by focusing on pragmatic economic goals, and by incanting denunciations of the "infamous gang of four" will suceed is as yet far from certain. So even totalitarian regimes quite obviously have their problems in manufacturing the *zeitgeist* they would choose for their peoples, a familiar "malfunction" which evidenced itself well before contemporary Communist China in such places as Nazi Germany, Fascist Italy, Stalin's Russia, and Franco's Spain.

regimes, and even then somewhat imperfectly. Democratic societies, including even those in which there is a high economic concentration of mass media ownership, are as a rule too pluralistic to produce the political conditions prerequisite for the effective exercise of such absolutist control.

So while it seems probable that the mass media will more and more come to furnish us the *stuff* of our nostalgias, it would be far-fetched to envision their being able to dictate and altogether manage the occasions and durations of our nostalgias. Perhaps the closest parallel in the field of collective behavior to this situation is the phenomenon of Fashion. As was pointed out long ago by Blumer[7], the Paris *haute couturier* and the New York garment industry simply cannot, contrary to what is sometimes charged by street cynics, decide and dictate by fiat what is to be worn and what shorn from one season to the next. Even if one were to assume some tacit trade conspiracy among the designers, the manufacturers, the fashion writers, and the merchandisers of new fashion—an extremely hazardous assumption in its own right—this still would prove extremely difficult to bring off. A very long list of bankruptcies and thousands of unsold "latest style" gowns (along with their "drastically reduced" accessories) attest to the pathetic failure of such pretended market omniscience and omnipotence. The collective stirrings, discontents, yearnings, and ambivalences upon which the acceptance of new fashions depends ultimately are, according to Blumer, simply too deep, too veiled, and too labile to permit a small group of designers, manufacturers, and merchandisers to "prescribe" with any degree of surety what is to be worn by the multitudes. Yet what comes to be worn does as a rule germinate from within this

[7]Herbert G. Blumer, "Collective Behavior," in A. M. Lee, ed., *New Outline of the Principles of Sociology* (New York: Barnes & Noble, 1946), pp. 216–218, and, more recently, the entry by Blumer on "Fashion," in David L. Sills, ed., *International Encyclopedia of the Social Sciences*, Vol. 5 (New York: Macmillan, 1968), pp. 341–345.

group, particularly from the designer whose "inspiration" may ignite the spark that eventually translates itself into a massively successful style change. But this still is more a matter of luck than willed outcome, more a case of the stylist's intuitively sensing the amorphous collective stirrings that his or her design may somehow capture and symbolically crystallize than of mechanically imposing one's own ideas on a passively receptive public.

As with fashion, the impulse to collective nostalgia also springs from vague mass stirrings, discontents, and yearnings, some of which were alluded to in previous chapters' discussion of the nostalgia wave of the nineteen-seventies. Not surprisingly, fashion often draws heavily on nostalgic feeling, although it would be mistaken to assume, as some do, that this is all that fashion is about—an endless replaying of styles from the past with only minor modifications from one revival to the next. Accordingly, much as the media might want or conceivably even conspire to schedule our future nostalgias, the same indeterminacies and mischances are bound to beset them as now do those who would impose a new fashion on the world. Are the vague mass stirrings being correctly apprehended? Do the ensuing stylistic interpretations provide a satisfying symbolic resolution to the tensions underlying the stirrings? And even prior to these questions, are the stirrings present at all and, if so, on a massive enough scale? These would, at best, be extremely elusive data to come by, and even if obtainable could not bestow on "conspirators" the necessary power and skill with which to successfully sell their preferred nostalgias to the rest of us.

Conclusion

"But," some readers are bound to object, "isn't it sufficient that media products have, as you yourself point out, come to dominate the landscape of our collective nostalgia? Is this not in itself dangerous enough, without worrying about anything so fanciful as whether media moguls can, at will, make or break particular nostalgia waves? Does this not further the same cultural debasement, the same plasticization, homogenization, and corruption of popular taste as the mass media are responsible for already? Indeed, is there not something particularly grim about the fact that in the modern world they have come to serve as not only the principal fount of our desires but the main repository of our memories as well? Who needs byzantine corporate conspiracies or clumsy dictatorial powers with this much going for them?"

These are, to be sure, complex and serious concerns which inevitably engage issues much broader than the future of nostalgia *per se*. Clearly, they cannot be disentangled from the many more awesome questions of the role of the mass media in modern society in general, a topic so vast and so rent with controversy as to carry it far beyond the modest confines of this book. But perhaps some few observations can be ventured, not as a definitive judgment on the matter, but by way of pointing to some useful avenues of approach to it.

First off, the reader may have noted a few paragraphs back that I indulged, with enough fulsomeness as to be suspect, in the familiar litany of deprecations of the mass media, referring to their ineluctable tendency to debase, corrupt, homogenize, and so forth—such being the charges leveled at them not only by the partisans of "high culture" but by Marxist and numerous conservative critics as well. But the exaggerated polemical tone of these remarks would lead one to wonder, is such actually the case, and can it be proved—assuming, that one can for empirical purposes first secure some consensus among critics on what is meant, for example, by "debased" or "elevated" tastes, no easy task in its own right?[8]

[8]Many of the arguments are ably and fairly summarized in Herbert J. Gans, *Popular Culture and High Culture* (New York: Basic Books, 1974), although Gans himself is a good deal more charitable than are most critics to the mass media and popular taste.

Despite almost a half-century of social science research on the effects of the mass media, we are still very much in the dark on the question of what difference they make and have made in the lives of people. To be sure, we know a great deal about their short-term, situationally bounded behavioral affects, about their ability to influence, for example, product purchases, candidate preferences, and, to an extent, opinion on leading political issues. But as to their long-term developmental, characterological, and cognitive effects—the ways in which they may have altered the fundamental perceptual categories through which we experience the world, or how they may have affected our sensibility and provided us with models of how to appear, act, and be—of such things we actually know remarkably little, in spite of the alacrity and certainty with which numerous critics are ready to pronounce on them in tones usually of apocalyptic despair. But it is precisely to this realm, to the murky nonverbal substratum of culture, that the issue of the media's debasement of nostalgic experience needs to be referred. In the absence of data it could perhaps be argued as persuasively—although it is not particularly fashionable to do so—that, rather than polluting the wells of our nostalgic memory, the mass media have enriched and invigorated them; that drawing upon the inspiration and talents of thousands, upon thousands of writers, producers, artists, and performers they have provided us with an infinitely greater variety of plots, thoughts, themes, ideas, and images than could have ever been generated from within the narrow boundaries of our own limited daily encounters and exchanges.

Are there, then, no cultural implications to be drawn from the circumstance that our future nostalgias, more than those of the past, are likely to be predominantly media-derived and media-borne, if not as outrightly manipulated perhaps as some fear? An answer, if there is one—and I am by no means certain that there is—would, it seems, have to reckon with the following tendencies and constraints, most of which have already been touched on in other connections.

140

Mass nostalgia reactions are most likely to occur in the wake of periods of severe cultural discontinuity, as happened following the profound identity upheavals of the nineteen-sixties. Nostalgia is also, as we have seen, a conserving influence; it juxtaposes the uncertainties and anxieties of the present with presumed verities and comforts of the lived past, although it would be incorrect to assume that because it does so it always arrests or inhibits present purpose and action. Depending on a variety of other collective circumstances and moods, it may "fail" altogether or hold present anxieties in check only slightly. Nevertheless, to the extent that future collective nostalgias will take their shape and substance increasingly from mass media representations, the nostalgic contents are likely to be more uniform, familiar, and, in the deepest sense, "known" to purveyor and recipient alike. Hence, the decision on whether or not to resort to nostalgic appeals either for crass commercial reasons or Machiavellian purposes of state can be subjected to more "rational" determination than in the past, when the silhouette of our individual nostalgias, particularly in a society as heterogeneous as America, tended to be more dissimilar and diverse. Given nostalgia's power as an emotion and the deep resonances it can activate among people, the temptation to "use" this now more calculable affective quantity by publicist, politician, and promotor is bound to be intensified. If nostalgic memories of the Glen Miller Band of 1942 can be placed in the service of a particular product, candidate, or political cause, what interested party will refrain from doing so?

A "politics of nostalgia" is, other things being equal, likely to assume a more prominent, though by no means dominant, place on the American political scene than it has until now, although David Riesman pointed out some twenty-five years ago it had by then already come to exert no small influence on public opinion formation and campaign rhetoric.[9] And in light of its conserving tendencies, its predilection to

[9] David Riesman, et al., *The Lonely Crowd* (New Haven: Yale University Press, 1940), pp. 184–209.

141

sustain continuities through the turbulence of rapid social change, a politics of nostalgia is also likely to act as something of a brake on the plethora of utopias emanating from the consciousness-raising, liberationist, and human potential movements of recent years. Whether this is good or bad, to be praised or condemned, is ultimately a question of political values and cannot be reduced to some simple calculation of costs and benefits. But that the mere capability for a more uniform and manageable resort to nostalgic sentiment in the politics of the future will *in and of itself* result in an undue strengthening of conservative forces or a reactionary perversion of the political process would seem to be a far-fetched and excessively pessimistic prognosis. Politics are simply too complex to permit such unilateral extrapolations from trends in one area of social life into politics' own much more comprehensive sphere. Indeed, even now it is interesting to see how, for example, a conservatively tinged nostalgia for "the beauties of the American wilderness and the out of doors" or "the abandoned Victorian mansions of the inner city" or "the old ethnic neighborhood with its distinctive customs" has combined with liberal preferences for central planning, corporate regulation, and controlled growth to result in political constituencies and platforms that are no longer so clearly liberal or conservative, Democratic or Republican, progressive or reactionary.

In regard then to the half-clever, half-disconcerting observation that nostalgia "ain't what it used to be," we finally have to agree "it surely ain't," just as at the turn of the century it no longer was what it had been when the Swiss physician Johannes Hofer first coined the term in 1688. But such is the way with words; they almost never are what they used to be, because experience is not what it used to be. On the other hand, to assume that, because of advanced developments in technology, communications, and organization, some incurable disease of the body politic mysteriously lurks in nostalgia's altered condition is as fanciful as it once was to attribute its cause to the rarefied Alpine air or the too-close, too-continuous clanging of cowbells.

142

INDEX

Index

145